D1090116

Saudi-Iranian Relations Since the Fall of Saddam

Rivalry, Cooperation, and Implications for U.S. Policy

Frederic Wehrey, Theodore W. Karasik, Alireza Nader, Jeremy Ghez, Lydia Hansell, Robert A. Guffey

Sponsored by the Smith Richardson Foundation

NATIONAL SECURITY RESEARCH DIVISION

The research described in this report was sponsored by the Smith Richardson Foundation and was conducted under the auspices of the International Security and Defense Policy Center within the RAND National Security Research Division (NSRD). NSRD conducts research and analysis for the Office of the Secretary of Defense, the Joint Staff, the Unified Commands, the defense agencies, the Department of the Navy, the Marine Corps, the U.S. Coast Guard, the U.S. Intelligence Community, allied foreign governments, and foundations.

Library of Congress Cataloging-in-Publication Data

Saudi-Iranian relations since the fall of Saddam : rivalry, cooperation, and implications
  for U.S. policy / Frederic Wehrey ... [et al.].
    p. cm.
  Includes bibliographical references.
  ISBN 978-0-8330-4657-4 (pbk. : alk. paper)
  1. Saudi Arabia—Foreign relations—Iran. 2. Iran—Foreign relations—Saudi
Arabia. 3. United States—Foreign relations—Persian Gulf States. 4. Persian Gulf
States—Foreign relations—United States. I. Wehrey, Frederic M.

  DS228.I7S28 2009
  327.538055—dc22

                                                                    2009008205

Cover photo courtesy of Getty Images. Photographed by Hassan Ammar.

The RAND Corporation is a nonprofit research organization providing objective analysis and effective solutions that address the challenges facing the public and private sectors around the world. RAND's publications do not necessarily reflect the opinions of its research clients and sponsors.
RAND® is a registered trademark.

Published 2009 by the RAND Corporation
1776 Main Street, P.O. Box 2138, Santa Monica, CA 90407-2138
1200 South Hayes Street, Arlington, VA 22202-5050
4570 Fifth Avenue, Suite 600, Pittsburgh, PA 15213-2665
RAND URL: http://www.rand.org/
To order RAND documents or to obtain additional information, contact
Distribution Services: Telephone: (310) 451-7002;
Fax: (412) 802-4981; Email: order@rand.org

Preface

The often tense relationship between Saudi Arabia and Iran has been at the center of many of the major political shifts that have occurred in the Middle East since the fall of Saddam Hussein in 2003. Changing diplomatic and economic arrangements in the Persian Gulf; the political upheaval in Lebanon; continuing strife in Palestine; and growing strategic concerns around the world about Iran's alleged pursuit of nuclear weapons have all, in some way, been shaped by the competing interests of these two nations. While it is not the sole contributor to these changes, understanding the Saudi-Iranian relationship will help U.S. policymakers discern the future contours of Middle East politics. This is especially important since Saudi Arabia and Iran will be the critical regional players in the wake of a U.S. drawdown and withdrawal from Iraq.

This report documents a study of Saudi-Iranian relations since 2003. It focuses on how the relationship has affected and been affected by the major events that have taken place in the Middle East. The research was conducted between fall 2006 and January 2009. It should be of interest to the policymaking community, defense analysts, and other observers of the Middle East.

This research was conducted within the International Security and Defense Policy Center (ISDP) of the RAND National Security Research Division (NSRD). NSRD conducts research and analysis for the Office of the Secretary of Defense, the Joint Staff, the Unified Combatant Commands, the defense agencies, the Department of the Navy, the Marine Corps, the U.S. Coast Guard, the U.S. Intelligence Community, allied foreign governments, and foundations.

For more information on RAND's International Security and Defense Policy Center, contact the Director, James Dobbins. He can be reached by email at James_Dobbins@rand.org; by phone at 703-413-1100, extension 5134; or by mail at the RAND Corporation, 1200 S. Hayes Street, Arlington, VA 22202. More information about RAND is available at www.rand.org.

Contents

Summary

The fall of Iraqi President Saddam Hussein in 2003 and the war in Iraq have affected sweeping changes in the strategic landscape of the Middle East, radically shifting the regional balance of power. Old security paradigms have been thrown into question, and local states appear to be reaffirming, renegotiating, or rethinking their relations with one another and with outside powers. Saudi Arabia and Iran have in many respects been the central players in this unfolding transformation. The dynamic relations between the two powers have affected the Persian Gulf, Iraq, Lebanon, and Palestine with important implications for regional stability and U.S. interests.

Bilateral Tensions Affect Regional Stability and U.S. Interests

Saudi Arabia and Iran are divided by long-standing structural tensions. Each has aspirations for Islamic leadership, and each possesses different visions of regional order. Whereas Tehran regards Riyadh as America's proxy and a buffer against Iran's rightful primacy in the Gulf, Saudi Arabia worries about Iran's asymmetric power and regional ambitions, especially its expanding influence in post-Saddam Iraq and its alleged pursuit of a nuclear weapon. A particular concern in Riyadh is Iran's ability to challenge the legitimacy of the al-Saud before regional and domestic audiences by upstaging them on pan-Arab issues such as Palestine.

The countries are further divided by political ideologies and governance. The philosophy of the Islamic Republic explicitly rejects the kinds of monarchical regimes seen in Saudi Arabia and other Arab states, legitimates the authority of the Iranian clerical elite, and incorporates quasi-democratic institutions. For their part, the rule of the al-Saud rests on their claim to custodianship of the Islamic holy sites in Mecca and Medina, dynastic privilege, a symbiotic but ultimately dominant relationship with the Saudi clerical class, and a celebration of the state-building achievements of Ibn Saud. Energy differences are a third source of tension. Whereas Saudi Arabia can afford to take a long-term view of the global oil market and has incentives to moderate prices, Iran is compelled by its smaller oil reserves and larger population to focus on high prices in the short term.

Together, these factors—along with the well-known sectarian and ethnic fissures that divide the Saudi and Iranian populations—would seem to predispose the two countries toward chronic hostility. Regional and Western commentators have warned of a Saudi-Iranian "proxy" conflict engulfing the region or a return to the ideological "Cold War" that marked the bilateral relationship after the 1979 Iranian Revolution.

Attempting to capitalize on the sources of enmity between the two states, the United States has thus far adopted a policy that tacitly endorses Saudi Arabia as an "Arab balancer" against Iran. This approach is based on the idea that the Sunni-Shi'a divide and other structural tensions naturally place Arab Gulf countries on one side of the equation and Iran on the other. The hope is that a bloc of "moderate Arab states," led by Saudi Arabia and sponsored by the United States, can check Iranian influence in the region.

Conventional Thinking About Saudi-Iranian Relations Must Be Reexamined

Yet the relationship between Saudi Arabia and Iran is more complex, dynamic, and multidimensional than the "bloc" approach seems to allow. This report documents a study by the RAND National Security

Research Division of how the bilateral relationship has shaped and been shaped by the political and ideological changes that have taken place since the fall of Saddam Hussein in 2003. The study concludes that conventional thinking about Saudi-Iranian relations must be reexamined. Four findings in particular challenge traditional assumptions:

The Sunni-Shi'a Divide Has Strained the Relationship, but It Is Not the Key Driver

Sectarian and ideological differences between the two states have had an "echo effect" on the region, but they are not the principal determinants in the policy outlook of each regime. The Sunni-Shi'a divide certainly factors into the calculus of the leadership and is either encouraged or downplayed as a tool in larger game of geopolitical maneuvering. Moreover, the leadership in each country must also contend with key constituents for whom sectarianism is deeply embraced, although this is more the case in Saudi Arabia than in Iran.

The Saudi regime faces pressure from Salafi clerics to take an anti-Shi'a position in its dealings with Iran, and in late 2006 there was indeed mounting Saudi public pressure to protect Sunnis in Iraq. At the same time, the ruling elite in Saudi Arabia appear to have exploited or tacitly endorsed this rhetoric as a way to counter the greater threat of Iran's pan-Islamist populism. Put differently, faced with a contender for symbolic leadership in the Middle East, Saudi Arabia has tried to paint Iran as a cultural and ideological aberration from the rest of the region, and the most expeditious means of doing this has been to cast the Islamic Republic's Shi'a/Persian ambitions as a threat to Sunnis everywhere. One unintended victim of this tactic has been Saudi Arabia's own Shi'a community.

For its part, Iran has tended to downplay sectarianism in the bilateral relationship, criticizing anti-Shi'a rhetoric from the Kingdom but often displaying recognition of the distinction between Saudi clerical voices and the Saudi regime. Moreover, the two states have at times taken steps to mitigate sectarian conflict in Lebanon and Iraq in order to pave the way for coordination on a range of economic and political issues.

The More Fundamental Disagreement Is over Regional Hierarchy and the Role of the United States

Since 2003, the fundamental driver of the relationship is a struggle to shape the regional balance of power. Each state sees the expansion of regional influence by the other as a net loss for itself, whether in Palestine, Lebanon, Iraq, or the Gulf littoral. This game of geopolitics is aided by the fact that the regional landscape is defined by weak states and contending local factions that invite outside meddling. In many cases, these factions line up along the Shi'a-Sunni divide, and thus Saudi and Iranian patronage invariably exacerbates a dangerous form of sectarian politics, whether or not this is the original intent of policymakers in Riyadh and Tehran.

In maneuvering on this landscape, Saudi Arabia and Iran wield asymmetrical policy tools; neither is likely to confront the other on the conventional battlefield. Iran is more adept at backing militant nonstate actors and playing a rejectionist trump card on issues such as Palestine and the U.S. presence in the region—a tactic that has formed an indirect critique of U.S.-allied regimes and in particular Gulf states that have adopted increasingly accommodating stances toward Israel. For its part, Saudi Arabia brings to bear greater financial resources, control of pan-Arab media outlets, and the backing of the region's key external power.

However, as we argue in this report, these attributes do not translate into greater regional legitimacy for the al-Saud or unwavering Arab consensus for Saudi leadership against Iran. Rather, quite the opposite may be true. Riyadh has therefore been careful to balance alignment with U.S. initiatives with its own unilateral diplomacy—both for symbolic reasons and because it has increasingly perceived U.S. policy toward Iran to be in disarray.

Containment of Iran by Saudi Arabia and the Gulf States Is Unrealistic

The notion of a watertight bloc of Gulf Arab states opposing Iran is therefore unrealistic, given the ambiguity about Saudi leadership, but also disunity within the Gulf Cooperation Council (GCC) and in particular the tendency of Qatar and Oman to go it alone. The tradition of bilateral dialogue between the individual Gulf states and Iran implicitly favors Tehran and has complicated Riyadh's efforts at confronting Iran. Moreover, Saudi Arabia has shown the tendency to accommodate and engage Iran in the Gulf when it perceives ambiguity and confusion in U.S. policy; the Saudi overture to Iran in the wake of the 2007 U.S. National Intelligence Estimate (NIE),[1] which was viewed in Riyadh as a downgrading of the Iranian threat, is a good example of this dynamic at work.

For its part, Tehran's posture toward Saudi Arabia and the Gulf has been affected by an internal debate between factions who see the Gulf as a zone of economic enrichment and multilateral diplomatic cooperation, and those who take a more hegemonic, proprietary view, preferring the instruments of intimidation and threat. It should be emphasized, however, that both sides in Tehran are united in the view that the U.S. presence as an external security guarantor should end—a view that is unacceptable to Saudi Arabia.

Iran Has Little Influence over Shi'as in Saudi Arabia and the Gulf, but Shi'a Marginalization Is a Continuing Concern

Despite these signs of accommodation in the Gulf, it is worth noting that the political marginalization and economic deprivation of Shi'a communities in Saudi Arabia's Eastern Province, Bahrain, and, to a lesser extent, Kuwait are potential flashpoints in the future. The Gulf Shi'as can hardly be considered "proxies" of Tehran; most regard the Islamic Republic with a degree of spiritual and emotional affinity but not as an object of political emulation. Yet more hard-line and radical elements may become empowered, particularly among the younger generation, if these communities continue to perceive a lack of progress on political inclusion, civil rights, and economic improvement.

---

[1] Office of the Director National Intelligence and the National Intelligence Council, *Iran: Nuclear Intentions and Capabilities*, November 2007.

Saudi Arabia and Iran Compete, Coordinate, and Engage in Different Arenas of the Middle East

The relationship between Saudi Arabia and Iran as it is evolving today appears to incorporate elements of both sectarian confrontation and pragmatic rapprochement. As in earlier periods (e.g., before the Iranian Revolution in 1979 and during the warming of relations in the mid-1990s), the two countries are showing their ability to reach an accommodation on regional order while minimizing deeper ideological and structural tensions. This hybrid approach plays out in different ways throughout the regions where the two countries come into contact—in Iraq, the Gulf, and the Levant.

Riyadh and Tehran Perceive Iraq as a Zero-Sum Game

Much focus has been directed at Iraq as an arena for "proxy" competition between Saudi Arabia and Iran, particularly in the event of a U.S. withdrawal. Saudi Arabia's previous warnings that it will increase its involvement in Iraq following a U.S. departure should not be dismissed. But its ability to support and influence Sunni factions should not be inflated, and its role in containing Iranian influence in Iraq may be more limited than is realized.

A key theme is Saudi Arabia's desire to keep the United States involved in Iraq as a balancer and, absent this, to play a role in shaping the outcome of any trilateral Iranian-U.S.-Iraqi talks. Sensing that this strategy may be eroding, Riyadh has recently taken steps to diversify and strengthen its contacts with a range of Iraqi political actors. Meanwhile, Iran has made overtures to Saudi Arabia about a sort of cooperative power-sharing relationship over Iraq that may mirror past coordination on Lebanon but that explicitly calls for the departure of U.S. forces. Riyadh likely sees this overture for what it is: an attempt to deprive Saudi Arabia of its external patron and relegate it to the status of junior partner in the new regional order. Instead of true cooperation, the Saudi-Iranian relationship over Iraq is likely to be defined as "managed rivalry," with a modicum of coordination and contact to prevent an escalation of sectarian conflict, which would benefit neither side.

Riyadh and Tehran Have Tried to Regulate Tensions over Iran's Nuclear Program

The advent of a nuclear-armed Iran would likely be perceived as an existential threat to Riyadh, possibly pushing Saudi Arabia to acquire its own countervailing deterrent. The Saudi reaction will likely be a key pivot around which the rest of the region's reactions will turn; interviews conducted by RAND researchers suggest widespread unease, particularly among smaller Gulf states, about Saudi Arabia's potential "overreaction" to the advent of a nuclear Iran. Current relations over the nuclear issue, however, are more muted than might be expected. In its approach, Riyadh appears to adhere more closely to the European line of treating the Iranian issue within the context of a WMD-free Middle East, which would include Israel. Such pronouncements are partly calculated to imply Riyadh's non-support for a U.S. strike, which Saudi Arabia perceives might engender domestic public opposition and erode the Kingdom's legitimacy on the Arab stage. Iran, for its part, appears to see the nuclear impasse as manageable. Through its official and unofficial press outlets, Iran has portrayed mutual harmony with Saudi Arabia on the issue, often citing what it perceives to be Riyadh's acceptance of the program's peaceful nature.

Rivalry in the Levant Is More Explicit

If Saudi-Iranian relations in the Gulf and Iraq are based on engagement and containment, respectively, then the Levant is best characterized as an arena for more open competition and rivalry. Much of this stems from Saudi perception of the Iranian threat. In the normative realm of Saudi public perception and belief in the legitimacy of the monarchy, Iran's actions in the Arab-Israeli sphere do far more harm to the al-Saud than its actions in Iraq. It was Hizballah's 2006 war with Israel that opened significant rifts inside Saudi policy circles and among the clerical elite and put the al-Saud in the awkward position of being upstaged on the Israeli-Palestinian issue by a non-Arab, Shi'a power. Riyadh also likely perceives that to keep its influence in the pan-Arab realm it must take a more proactive stance on the Israeli-Palestinian issue, as well as Lebanon.

Riyadh is currently focused on trying to isolate and weaken Syria since the assassination of Lebanese Prime Minister Rafik Hariri, while tacitly supporting the Turkish-Israeli effort to pry Damascus from Iran's orbit and lure it back to the Arab fold. In response, Iran has attempted to paint Saudi policies as explicitly sectarian in nature in order to discredit its role as a broker, either on the Israeli-Palestinian issue or in Lebanon. The Iranian press has highlighted Riyadh's support to radical Salafi groups and has gone so far as to implicate it in the assassination of Hizballah commander Imad Mughniyah.

An important dimension of the relationship in the Levant is the way it conditions the views of local actors, particularly in Lebanon; outside meddling and interference has been used by competing Lebanese factions as justification for avoiding compromise.

Implications for U.S. Policy

Incorporating the themes outlined above, U.S. policy can better manage the implications of the Saudi-Iranian relationship in the following ways:

View Saudi Arabia Less as a Bulwark Against Iran and More as an Interlocutor

U.S.-Saudi interests are aligned against Iran in many ways, but Riyadh is unlikely to act in lockstep with Washington's strategy. Indeed, the current Saudi-centric containment strategy appears to have been overtaken by events, with the Kingdom pursuing a nuanced approach that incorporates elements of accommodation, engagement, and rollback. A U.S. paradigm that views Saudi Arabia as a confrontational proxy against Iran, with the expectation that Riyadh will employ all levers of influence at its disposal, does not reflect regional reality or the pattern of interaction between the two states. Riyadh has a demonstrated tendency to hedge its bets, to avoid taking stark policy decisions, and to keep multiple options open—especially in the context of what it perceives as inconsistent and ambiguous U.S. policies toward Iran.

In this light, recommendations that Riyadh confront China and Europe to sever their business ties with Iran or risk losing economic access to the Kingdom are probably not viable options for exerting multilateral pressure on Iran's nuclear ambitions. Moreover, regional observers see little role for Saudi Arabia as a real balancer against Iran, but rather view it as a critical pillar in a diplomatic vanguard that includes Egypt and Jordan. Some voices in Saudi Arabia appear to appreciate the Kingdom's role as an interlocutor between Iran and the United States, although the leadership in Riyadh remains fundamentally fearful of an eventual U.S.-Iranian reconciliation. The United States should seek to cultivate Saudi moves toward dialogue, encouraging Saudi outreach to Tehran while at the same time working to resolve the arenas of competition between the two states, particularly on the Arab-Israeli front.

Much of this depends on a unilateral de-escalation of U.S. rhetoric on Iran, combined with U.S. endorsement of a broader Gulf engagement with Tehran. If the Saudis perceive that the weight of regional and U.S. diplomacy is geared toward dialogue, they would have strong incentives to play a key role, lest smaller Arab states outbid them. However, a muddled U.S. approach to Iran along with frequently confrontational rhetoric plays into the hands of more hard-line factions in Riyadh who eschew engagement.

Seek Saudi Burden-Sharing in Iraq, but Not to Counteract Iran

As noted above, it is important that the United States not exaggerate Saudi Arabia's influence over Sunni factions in Iraq or view it as analogous to Iran's influence. The Saudis themselves appear to recognize this and are diversifying the breadth and intensity of their contacts with a wide range of Iraqi political factions. The United States should encourage this trend, but with the understanding that these levers should work toward the stabilization and equitable political development of Iraq, rather than the targeted rollback of Iranian influence. Already, Tehran is alarmed that the Sunni tribal strategy employed in al-Anbar against al-Qaeda could be replicated among southern Shi'a tribes against Iranian influence, and it likely views Saudi Arabia as a potential patron in this effort, despite the sectarian divide. Taken together with Tehran's long-standing perception of Riyadh's incitement of Sunni volunteers to Iraq, this could significantly exacerbate tensions, with destabilizing consequences for Iraq and the broader region.

It is ultimately the Iraqi government and public who will determine the type and scope of Iranian influence over Iraq's political, economic, and social affairs. One of the important indigenous buffers to Iranian interference is Iraqi nationalism, which appears to be asserting itself in light of growing public intolerance for Iran's lethal support to Shi'a militias in mid-2008, the ratification of the U.S.-Iraq Strategic Framework Agreement (SFA) in November 2008, and the defeat of the Iranian-backed Islamic Supreme Council of Iraq (ISCI) in the January 2009 provincial elections. Taking this into account, Washington should expend great effort to allay Saudi fears about Iran's actual and future influence over Iraqi Shi'as.

To do this, the United States must carefully set the stage for the drawdown of U.S. forces—providing necessary security guarantees to Riyadh yet also communicating to the Iraqi government the importance of building institutions in a nonsectarian manner, particularly the Iraqi Security Forces, and integrating the Sunni-based Awakening Councils and Sons of Iraq into Iraqi political life. In light of these confidence-building measures, Saudi Arabia must be encouraged to expand its diplomatic contacts with Iraq, as with any neighboring country. Most specifically, Saudi Arabia must be encouraged to open an embassy in Baghdad. This would signal to Iran the necessity of acknowledging the country's links to the Sunni west, normalizing its relations with Iraq, and ending its policy of lethal aid to Shi'a militias.

Encourage Saudi Initiatives on the Arab-Israeli Front

This study argues that Iran's threat to Saudi Arabia is not necessarily as a conventional military power but rather as a state that seeks to symbolically challenge the Kingdom's claim to leadership on Arab issues, particularly on Palestine. Iran's militant nonstate allies are players in this strategy, dependent on Syria as a key conduit. Much of the focus by Saudi Arabia is geared toward eliminating this conduit by wrestling Syria away from Tehran. Yet Riyadh is unlikely to find a compromise with Damascus on the Hariri issue, and, given the durability and robustness of the Tehran-Damascus axis, energy might be better expended on other areas. Specifically, regional peace initiatives such as that put forward by Saudi King Abdullah are proactive efforts that help isolate Iranian rejectionism on the Arab-Israeli front, even if they ultimately fall short of achieving a lasting peace. Washington should be cognizant, however, of how intra-Arab rivalries, particularly within the GCC, can undermine Saudi initiatives on the Palestine issue and against Iran.

Push for Domestic Reform in Saudi Arabia and the Gulf to Mitigate Sectarianism

The sectarian dimension of Saudi-Iran relations partly stems from political inequity among the Gulf Shi'as and fears by Riyadh and other Sunni regimes that these populations are susceptible to Iranian influence. The mid-1990s have shown that genuine efforts toward integration and dialogue between rulers and their Shi'a populations has the effect of lessening Iran's attractiveness as an external patron. Conversely, the hardening of anti-Shi'a discrimination and backtracking on reforms could make Shi'a public opinion swing more toward more radical domestic factions who are influenced by Iran or who seek to emulate the Hizballah model in the Gulf. More equitable power sharing, in which hard-line Salafi clerics are prevented from airing their anti-Shi'a views, will also improve Saudi-Iranian bilateral relations and reduce sectarian tensions.

Ultimately, the United States and regional governments must acknowledge that the threat of an Iranian-backed Shi'a fifth column in the Gulf is overblown, but that stagnation on reform and rights toward the Shi'as could make these fears a self-fulfilling prophecy. Washington should avoid viewing sectarian tension as an inevitable feature of the bilateral relationship, but rather recognize such tension as a by-product of fundamental power inequities in the Gulf that can be improved through reform. At the same time, the United States should understand that the scope and pace of any reforms will be determined by the Gulf states themselves.

Avoid Actions That Inflame Iranian Perceptions of External Meddling in Its Affairs

Iran has great reason to fear external meddling in its internal affairs, particularly given a long pattern of historical interference by Western powers, of which the most notorious is the 1953 coup against Prime Minister Mohammed Mossadegh.[2] The fall of Saddam has only heightened this perception, and Tehran fears that a decentralized Iraq could increase dissent among the ethnic and sectarian groups within its own borders. The Sunnis in Baluchestan and the Arabs in Khuzestan are potential concerns, as is Iran's perception of a Saudi role in agitating both populations. While much of this fear is undoubtedly exaggerated, Washington can mitigate it as a source of Saudi-Iranian tension by abandoning the idea that domestic dissent inside Iran can be engineered from the outside. If, on the other hand, this idea grows, the potential for what one Saudi interlocutor called a "dirty war" escalating among proxy groups outside the territories of each country could grow, to the detriment of U.S. interests and regional stability.

Pursue Saudi-Iranian Endorsement of Multilateral Security for the Gulf

This study found that the Gulf is one arena where bilateral tensions have been regulated by a host of shared interests. Capitalizing on this dynamic, the United States should work toward a more cooperative Gulf security arrangement that recognizes Iran as a valid player but assuages Saudi and Gulf concerns about Iranian dominance. A conflict-regulating "concert" system, like the Organization for Security and Cooperation in Europe (OSCE), bears further consideration in this regard. In this sort of forum, mutual threat perceptions are aired and conflict-reduction measures are pursued. Cooperation in the maritime area would be a useful area of focus for such a forum (such as work on a regional incidents-at-sea agreement), particularly given the potential for miscalculation and escalation in critical waterways, such as the Strait of Hormuz.

This proposed structure is not without its drawbacks: The Saudi preference for an external, nonregional security guarantor has been

---

[2] The coup was orchestrated by the CIA and Britain's Secret Intelligence Service (SIS).

noted, and Iran is suspicious that such proposals are merely a cover for increased U.S. hegemony. Smaller Gulf states, such as Oman and Qatar, are unlikely to join until the future of Iraq is secured, and many will continue their preference for bilateral ties with the United States, fearful of Saudi Arabia's dominance. In addition, the GCC's internal political tensions, such as Shi'a marginalization, make the implementation of this structure more problematic; as we have seen, much of the Gulf states' threat perception of Iran is a mirror of domestic regime insecurity. Thus, internal reform and liberalization remain key priorities.

Despite these obstacles, a new paradigm that does not focus on a specific threat, but rather provides an open-ended security forum in which regional states can discuss and address a range of challenges, stands a better chance than a more traditional balancing approach that imparts too much confidence in Riyadh's will and capabilities to act as a true counterweight to Iran.

Acknowledgments

We would like to thank Nadia Schadlow and Marin Strmecki of the Smith Richardson Foundation for their support throughout this research. We would also like to thank the librarians, contract administrators, and administrative assistants at RAND; our numerous interlocutors in the field; and our colleagues for their support. In particular, we thank Brian Nichiporuk, Jerry Green, Steve Simon, Greg Gause, John Limbert, Toby Craig Jones, Dalia Dassa Kaye, Nadia Oweidat, Peter A. Wilson, Larry Rubin, the anonymous reviewers at the Smith Richardson Foundation, Isabel Sardou, Christine Galione, and Roberta Shanman. RAND editors Lynn Rubenfeld and James Torr adroitly guided the study through the production process. Finally, we are grateful to James F. Dobbins, director of the International Security and Defense Policy Center, for his guidance and encouragement.

Abbreviations

AWACS	Airborne Warning and Control System
CIA	Central Intelligence Agency
GCC	Gulf Cooperation Council
IAEA	International Atomic Energy Agency
IFLB	Islamic Front for the Liberation of Bahrain
IRGC	Islamic Revolutionary Guards Corps
NIE	National Intelligence Estimate
NPT	Nuclear Non-Proliferation Treaty
OIC	Organization of the Islamic Conference
OIR	Organization for the Islamic Revolution on the Arabian Peninsula
OPEC	Organization of Petroleum Exporting Countries
OSCE	Organization for Security and Cooperation in Europe
UAE	United Arab Emirates

CHAPTER ONE

Introduction: Saudi Arabia and Iran—Between Confrontation and Cooperation

The fall of Iraqi President Saddam Hussein in 2003 and the war in Iraq have affected sweeping changes to the strategic landscape of the Middle East, radically shifting the regional balance of power. Old security paradigms have been thrown into question, and local states appear to be reaffirming, renegotiating, or rethinking their relations with one another and with outside powers. Relations between Saudi Arabia and Iran have arguably been a central pivot around which this transformation has turned. The collapse of Iraq as the eastern flank of the Arab world and growing regional perceptions of U.S. immobility have encouraged Tehran's ambitions for regional preeminence, amplified its existing influence, and provoked a Sunni Arab diplomatic counterreaction, spearheaded to a large degree by Saudi Arabia and tacitly endorsed by Washington.[1] The dynamic relations between the two

---

[1] For analysis of Iran's influence and calculations in the region post-Iraq, see Robert Lowe and Claire Spencer, eds., *Iran: Its Neighbors and the Regional Crises*, Royal Institute of International Affairs, Chatham House, 2006; and Anoushiravan Ehteshami, "Iran's International Posture After the Fall of Baghdad," *Middle East Journal*, Vol. 58, No. 2, Spring 2004. For the Saudi reaction, see Michael M. Slackman and Hassan M. Fattah, "In Public View, Saudis Counter Iran in Region," *The New York Times*, 6 February 2007. For a brief overview, see Lionel Beehner, "Iran's Saudi Counterweight," Council on Foreign Relations, 16 March 2007.

powers are unfolding in the Persian Gulf, Iraq, Lebanon, and Palestine, with important implications for regional stability and U.S. interests.[2]

Deep Bilateral Tensions Affect Regional Stability and U.S. Interests

Long-standing structural tensions would appear to characterize much of the relationship between these oil-rich powers, each possessing aspirations for Islamic leadership and differing visions of regional order. Tehran continues to regard Riyadh as America's principal local proxy and a buffer against Iran taking what it feels is its rightful place as the region's preeminent power.[3] From its perspective, Saudi Arabia harbors a deep-seated distrust of Iran, stemming from the 1979 Revolution and its explicit call for overturning the Sunni monarchical order. Yet even before this ideological challenge, Riyadh long perceived a stark asymmetry between its own national power and that of Iran, in terms of demography, industrial capacity, and military strength. The recent growth of Iranian influence in Shi'a-dominated Iraq and Tehran's nuclear aspirations are seen in Riyadh as catastrophically upsetting the balance-of-power equation that had favored Saudi Arabia for more than 20 years.[4] More distantly, the prospect of Iranian-U.S. rapprochement

---

[2] For an Iranian view of how this struggle is playing out, see "Ruyarui-e Iran va Arabestan dar khavar-e miane [Iran and Saudi Arabia Confrontation in the Middle East]," *Aftab News*, 5 December 2006.

[3] In the aftermath of revolution, Iranian officials went so far as to decry Wahhabism, the dominant form of Islam in Saudi Arabia, as "America's Islam."

[4] Interviews with Saudi government officials in Riyadh and Jeddah, 2006. See also F. Gregory Gause III, "Saudi Arabia: Iraq, Iran and the Regional Power Balance and the Sectarian Question," *Strategic Insights,* February 2007a. Saudi preoccupation with Iraq achieved considerable notoriety with the publication of an op-ed by a semi-official analyst; see Nawaf Obaid, "Stepping into Iraq: Saudi Arabia Will Protect Sunnis If the U.S. Leaves," *The Washington Post*, 26 November 2006b. The debate over Saudi intervention is covered in Megan Stack, "Hands Off or Not? Saudis Wring Theirs over Iraq," *The New York Times*, 24 May 2006.

(or even near-term coordination on Iraq) would appear to jeopardize the privileged position Riyadh has long enjoyed in Gulf affairs.[5]

The regimes in Riyadh and Tehran are buttressed by disparate political ideologies: Governance in Saudi Arabia rests on a careful symbiosis with the clerical establishment, but accords ultimate authority to the al-Saud dynasty based on their claim to custodianship of the Islamic holy sites in Mecca and Medina and their genealogical ties to the founder of the Kingdom, Ibn Saud. Iran's Khomeinist ideology is vehemently anti-monarchical, formalizes clerical authority in politics and—especially under President Mahmoud Ahmadinejad—trumpets an explicitly populist line.[6] Iran has also rattled Saudi Arabia and other Arab states through its "Arab street" strategy of speaking directly over the heads of Arab rulers to their publics, undermining the rulers' legitimacy by portraying them as sclerotic lackeys of Washington, and upstaging them on the Palestinian question through provocative rhetoric and support to such groups as Hamas and Hizballah.[7]

Economically, the two states have differing agendas at the Organization of Petroleum Exporting Countries (OPEC) that stem from their disparate economic needs and demography. Saudi Arabia has the largest proven reserves in the world and is a major supplier to the Far

---

[5] Kirk Semple, "Sunni Leaders Say U.S.-Iran Talks Amount to Meddling," *The New York Times*, 18 March 2006; Tariq al-Humayd, "Ala Matha Tufawad Washington Tehran? [What Will Washington Negotiate with Tehran?]," *al-Sharq al-Awsat*, 15 October 2007b; "Trilateral Talks Rattle Gulf States While Concealing Complex Iranian Dynamics," *Gulf States Newsletter*, Vol. 31, No. 807, 8 June 2007.

[6] Saleh al-Mani, "The Ideological Dimension in Saudi-Iranian Relations," in Jamal S. al-Suwaidi, *Iran and the Gulf: A Search for Stability,* Abu Dhabi, Emirates Center for Strategic Studies and Research, 1996, pp. 158–174.

[7] As noted by Olivier Roy in *The Failure of Political Islam* (Cambridge, Mass.: Harvard Belknap Press, 2001, p. 123), Iran's Arab strategy is not reflective of its expansive influence but rather a symptom of its fundamental isolation. By being "more Arab than the Arabs," Iran is trying to, as noted by Roy, "break out of the Shi'a ghetto." See also Morten Valbjørn and André Bank, "Signs of a New Arab Cold War: The 2006 Lebanon War and the Sunni-Shi'i Divide," *Middle East Report,* Spring 2007; Andrew England, "Arab Street Warms to Showman Ahmadi-Nejad," *Financial Times*, 6 April 2007; Zogby International, "Middle East Opinion: Iran Fears Aren't Hitting the Arab Street," 2006; and Renud Girard, "The Calculated Provocations of the Islamist Iranian President," *Le Figaro* (Paris), 19 December 2005.

East, the United States, and the rest of the world. It is therefore more willing to take a long-term view of the oil market. Iran, with its lower oil reserves and larger population, shows far less concern over the long-term oil market and faces more dire immediate requirements than Saudi Arabia.[8]

Taken in sum, these factors—along with the well-known sectarian and ethnic fissures that divide the two states' populations—have generated concern among U.S. policymakers and security analysts. Regional and Western commentators have warned of a Saudi-Iranian "proxy" conflict engulfing the region or a return to the ideological "Cold War" that marked the bilateral relationship after the 1979 Revolution.[9] Many observers have already interpreted outbreaks of regional instability as being incited, or even orchestrated, by these two powers seeking to outmaneuver one another—in Iraq, Gaza, and Lebanon.

Conventional Thinking About Saudi-Iranian Relations Must Be Reexamined

U.S. policy thus far appears to be focused not on mitigating the sources of these bilateral tensions, but rather on seeking to use Saudi Arabia

---

[8] "OPEC Blunder Reveals Saudi-Iran Disagreement on Dollar," *Agence France-Presse*, 17 November 2007.

[9] See Y. Mansharof, H. Varulkar, D. Lav, and Y. Carmon, "The Middle East on a Collision Course (4): Saudi/Sunni-Iranian/Shiite Conflict-Diplomacy and Proxy Wars," *Middle East Media Research Institute (MEMRI)*, Inquiry and Analysis Series, No. 324, 9 February 2007; and Iason Athanasiadis, "Sectarian Battles Spill Beyond Iraq; Sunnis, Shiites Eye Spoils for a Cold War Victory," *Washington Times*, 13 December 2006. For the "spillover" from Iraq, see Daniel L. Byman and Kenneth Pollack, *Things Fall Apart: Containing the Spillover from an Iraqi Civil War*, Brookings Institution, Saban Center for Middle East Policy, January 2007. A less extreme view is found in Augustus Richard Norton, "The Shiite 'Threat' Revisited," *Current History,* December 2007. Norton writes, "Reverberations from the 2003 invasion of Iraq may last for decades. But an inexorable spread of Sunni-Shi'a conflict is only the worse case, and frankly it is not very likely." See also Joost Hiltermann, "Iraq and the New Sectarianism in the Middle East," synopsis of a presentation at the Massachusetts Institute of Technology, 12 November 2006; Omayma Abd al-Latif, "The Shia-Sunni Divide: Myths and Reality," *Al-Ahram Weekly*, 1–7 March 2007; and Toby Craig Jones, "Saudi Arabia's Not So New Anti-Shi'ism," *Middle East Report,* Vol. 242, Spring 2007, pp. 29–32).

as an "Arab balancer" against Iran. This view is encouraged by the idea that the Sunni-Shi'a divide naturally places the Arab states of the Persian Gulf on one side of the equation and Iran on the other. Yet relations between the two powers are complex and multidimensional, and a number of assumptions deserve to be reexamined, particularly regarding the confrontational nature of their policies and the sectarian component.

First, the presumption of a watertight bloc of "moderate Arab states," led by Saudi Arabia, sponsored by the United States, and acting in lockstep against Iranian influence should not be taken as an accurate representation of facts on the ground.[10] It is true that Sunni Arab fears of Iran have at times strengthened regional support for Saudi Arabia's activism in the region. Yet the specter of Iranian influence and Saudi Arabia's resulting assertiveness has also intensified long-standing inter-Arab debates between the Gulf and the Levant and within the Gulf Cooperation Council (GCC) about regional hierarchy, sovereignty, and the degree of accommodation that is permissible with Tehran. For the smaller Gulf states and for Egypt, Riyadh's new activism may be equally as alarming as the threat from Iran itself.[11]

Secondly, Saudi Arabia's region-wide strategy toward Iran appears to be more nuanced than a simple "blocking" action; it incorporates elements of rollback, containment, and engagement that are playing out simultaneously in a number of subregions in the Middle East. When necessary, the two states have also shown the propensity for

---

[10] For Gulf Arab wariness of both the United States and Iran, see Neil Partrick, "Dire Straits for US Mideast Policy: The Gulf Arab States and US-Iran Relations," *Royal United Services Institute Commentary*, 9 January 2008. For a discussion of recent Saudi and Gulf engagement of Iran, see Charles Kupchan and Ray Takeyh, "Iran Just Won't Stay Isolated," *Los Angeles Times*, 4 March 2008.

[11] For Egyptian fears of a possible Saudi-Iranian rapprochement and Egypt's general loss of stature on pan-Arab affairs, see "Cairo Political Analysts View Implications of Iranian-Saudi Rapprochement," *al-Misr al-Yawm* (Cairo), translated by Open Source Center, GMP20070309007003, 9 March 2007; and Khalid al-Dakhil, "al-Taakul al-Dawr al-Misri fi al-Mintaqa [The Erosion of the Egyptian Role in the Region]," *al-Arabiya.net*, 5 July 2006. For Arab and especially Saudi reactions to a possible Iranian nuclear capability, see Dalia Dassa Kaye and Frederic M. Wehrey, "A Nuclear Iran: The Reactions of Neighbours," *Survival*, Vol. 49, No. 2, Summer 2007.

pragmatic cooperation in specific geographic areas and on issues where their interests intersect—even if in other areas there is concurrently open rivalry. Such calculations often take place independently of U.S. pressure or encouragement. As discussed further in this report, Saudi-Iranian efforts to mediate sectarian tensions in Lebanon following the 2006 Lebanon war provide the best illustration of this cooperation and showcase the way the two states attempt to lend themselves an aura of indispensability to local actors.[12] Yet Hizballah's move into West Beirut in the spring of 2008 also demonstrates how local dynamics can quickly undermine the efforts of these regional powers.

Finally, sectarianism should not be overstated as a factor in the two countries' policy calculus toward one another.[13] The religious foundations of each regime's legitimacy make it unsurprising that Sunni-Shi'a tensions are a factor in the relationship, and there is indeed sectarian partisanship among segments of the citizenry, particularly within the clerical establishment of each country.[14] Yet official pronouncements are surprisingly calibrated and carefully worded on these issues. Saudi

---

[12] "Saudi Foreign Minister on Lebanon, Iraq, Sectarian Issues," *al-Arabiya Television,* Open Source Center Feature, FEA20070129084306, 25 January 2007; Michael Slackman, "Iran and Saudi Arabia Mediating in Lebanon Crisis," *International Herald Tribune,* 30 January 2007a; Michael Slackman, "Iran and Saudi Arabia Mediate in Lebanon Crisis as U.S. Looks on," *The New York Times,* 31 January 2007b.

[13] For seminal work on sectarianism as a feature of the new regional landscape, see Vali Nasr, *The Shi'a Revival: How Conflicts Within Islam Will Shape the Future,* New York: W.W. Norton, 2005; Yizhak Nakash, *Reaching for Power: The Shi'a in the Modern Arab World,* Princeton, N.J.: Princeton University Press, 2006; Juan Cole, "A Shi'a Crescent? The Regional Impact of the Iraq War," *Current History,* Vol. 105, No. 687, January 2006; and Jones (2007). Jones writes, "Unlike in the 1980s, when Saudi Arabia met the ideological threat posed by Khomeini head on, the kingdom's rulers have not consistently manipulated sectarian hostility or consistently adopted a confrontational posture toward Iran, despite their clear desire to check or roll back Iranian influence."

[14] In Saudi Arabia, the clerical establishment is the wellspring for much of this. In mid-2007, however, the Kingdom has taken tentative and perhaps temporary steps to curtail anti-Shi'a and pro-jihad *fatawa* (pronouncements); Iran's Arabic-language TV station *al-Alam* took the remarkable step of applauding an anti-jihad *fatwa* by the Grand Mufti of Saudi Arabia, Abd al-Aziz al-Shaykh. See "Saudi Mufti Warns Against Joining Jihad Abroad," Saudi Press Agency (Riyadh), translated by Open Source Center, GMP20071002825008, 1 October 2007.

King Abdullah, for example, noted in an interview that Sunni-Shi'a tensions are a "matter of concern, not a matter of danger."[15] Iranian officials are also careful to avoid demonizing Sunni Arabs as a whole, focusing instead on anti-Shi'a Sunni extremists. As discussed further in this report, it is more in keeping with Iran's ideological aims to emphasize the divide between the "Arab street" and the monarchy than divisions within Islam.

Political factionalism, on the other hand, is certainly a factor in the bilateral relationship; it sends mixed signals to the other side and complicates efforts at dialogue.[16] Given the opacity of decision-making inside Iran and Saudi Arabia, it is difficult to accurately discern the policy views of different personalities and groups. Yet during key junctures since 2003, factional differences have risen to the fore. In Saudi Arabia, for example, two trends appear to have vied over Iran policy: a more hostile one embodied by Prince Bandar bin Sultan and a more conciliatory one advanced by King Abdullah. As the Kingdom's national security advisor and ex-ambassador to the United States, Bandar reportedly coordinated closely with the U.S. administration on a more confrontational policy designed to build regional consensus against Iran. In late 2006, this effort provoked the resignation of Prince Turki al-Faysal, the Saudi ambassador to the United States, who, it is said, disagreed with Bandar's approach in favor of greater diplomacy and engagement with Tehran. By March 2007, however, the factions appear to have coalesced behind King Abdullah's more nuanced approach, which involved publicly distancing the Kingdom from U.S. policy, offering lukewarm support for the U.S.-sponsored GCC+2 (Egypt and Jordan) coalition against Iran, and simultaneously pursuing a more unilateral diplomacy in the Levant and the Gulf.[17]

---

[15] Interview with King Abdullah in *al-Siyasa* (Kuwait), January 27, 2008.

[16] For a discussion of the domestic drivers of Saudi foreign policy, see Gerd Nonneman, "Determinants and Patterns of Saudi Foreign Policy: 'Omnibalancing' and 'Relative Autonomy' in Multiple Environments," in Paul Aarts and Gerd Nonneman, eds., *Saudi Arabia in the Balance: Political Economy, Society, Foreign Affairs*, New York: New York University Press, 2005, pp. 315–351.

[17] Hassan M. Fattah, "Bickering Saudis Struggle for an Answer to Iran's Rising Influence in the Middle East," *The New York Times*, 22 December 2006. Also, Marina Ottaway,

All of these considerations suggest that U.S. policymakers should take a fresh look at the relationship between these pivotal players and how it might affect U.S. interests in the future.

This Study Helps Fill an Important Policy Gap

Few studies have attempted to grapple with the important shifts in Saudi-Iranian relations since the U.S. invasion of Iraq in 2003.[18] There is a critical need for a policy-relevant approach that focuses on the sources of tension *and* cooperation between the two powers, and the implications of this dynamism for both regional stability and U.S. policy. Similarly, few treatments have canvassed the full range of policy levers—diplomatic, economic, media, cultural and religious, and military/intelligence-related—that the two states wield in their bilateral relations. Understanding how these instruments are deployed for confrontation or collusion in various areas in the Middle East is critical for drawing broader implications for U.S. policy, particularly concerning Iran.

This report helps to fill this gap with a fresh assessment of Saudi-Iranian relations after the fall of Saddam Hussein. The methodology is grounded in a combination of primary sources and fieldwork. We pay special attention to indigenous media sources in the region, focusing in particular on how editorials from the state-sponsored press in Saudi Arabia and Iran offer clues about regime perceptions of sectarian strife and bilateral competition.

Aside from these text-based approaches, the study relies on fieldwork conducted in Saudi Arabia, Bahrain, Kuwait, the United Arab Emirates (UAE), Lebanon, Egypt, and Jordan from 2006 to 2008. During this period, we captured a range of viewpoints from government

---

"The New Arab Diplomacy: Not with the U.S. and Not Against the U.S.," *Carnegie Papers*, Number 94, Washington, D.C.: Carnegie Endowment for International Peace, July 2008.

[18] Exceptions include Gause (2007a) and Banafsheh Keynoush, *The Iranian-Saudi Arabian Relationship: From Ideological Confrontation to Pragmatic Accommodation*, doctoral dissertation at the Fletcher School of Law and Diplomacy, Tufts University, Medford, Mass., 2007.

officials, diplomats, military officers, and think tanks. Our analysis is also informed by views of Saudi-Iranian relations from nonofficial actors in a number of countries: political oppositionists, religious figures, and journalists.

Taking these sources into account, our study unfolds in the following structure:

- **Chapter Two** discusses sectarianism and ideology as sources of contention between Saudi Arabia and Iran. It analyzes the extent to which these divisions affect each state's regional aspirations, threat perceptions, and behavior.
- **Chapter Three** explores Saudi-Iranian relations within the Gulf "Core" (the Gulf Arab states and Iraq) since 2003. Special attention is devoted to understanding how smaller Gulf states perceive their position in the context of Saudi-Iranian relations.
- **Chapter Four** examines the implications of Saudi-Iranian relations for the Levant (particularly Lebanon and Palestine).
- **Chapter Five** summarizes our findings and presents recommendations for U.S. policymakers.

CHAPTER TWO

Sectarianism and Ideology in the Saudi-Iranian Relationship

As noted in Chapter One, the conventional narrative of Saudi-Iranian relations suggests that heightened Sunni-Shi'a tensions throughout the Middle East should be a significant factor in the policy calculus of each regime. Ideologies that emphasize the distinctions between Arabs and Persians, the East and the West, and ruling classes and the "street" are also thought to inform Saudi and Iranian threat perceptions. While these structural elements certainly affect relations between Saudi Arabia and Iran, they are not the main drivers. Rather, sectarianism and ideology function both as calculated instruments of state policy and as a set of deeply held beliefs by certain key constituencies that decisionmakers must factor into their policy calculus.

We begin by outlining the background of Saudi-Iranian relations to understand how each regime has traditionally viewed its place in the regional order and shaped its policies accordingly.

We then examine Iran's "Arab street" strategy as an ideological component of its foreign policy that has had the effect of indirectly undercutting the al-Saud and, more broadly, Sunni Arab regimes in the Middle East. This tactic reached its height with the July 2006 war in Lebanon, which provoked debate inside the Kingdom and a flurry of anti-Iranian and anti-Shi'a invective from Saudi clerical figures. The following two sections examine the consequences of this sectarian response for Saudi Arabia's Shi'a population and Iran's Sunni population.

Finally, we address how the two states have recently sought to dampen sectarian tensions.

For U.S. policymakers, understanding the religious and ideological sources of confrontation and cooperation is critical to managing the Saudi-Iranian relationship and mitigating instability throughout the region. A policy that either knowingly or inadvertently attaches too much weight to these sectarian and ideological factors—in effect conflating the *symbolic vocabulary* of the bilateral relationship with its *substance*—could actually provoke greater tensions and potential conflict.

Post-Saddam Relations Unfold Against a Turbulent Backdrop

Saudi-Iranian relations are unfolding today against the backdrop of a post-1979 ebb and flow of ideological contention and pragmatic rapprochement.[1] Understanding this fluctuation is important for discerning the variable drivers for bilateral relations: Perceptions of U.S. policy, leadership changes and domestic factionalism, and regional conflict all combine to exert influence. As noted by a Gulf commentator, relations between Saudi Arabia and Iran are frequently the result of the "echo of (regional) changes, rather than an expression of national interests."[2] Analyzing the pre-1979 period also yields fruitful insights into how each state, irrespective of the complexion of its regime, views its place in the regional order.

Under the Shah during the 1960s, the two states shared mutual security concerns about the anti-monarchist and pan-Arab platform of Egyptian president Gamal Abd al-Nasser. There was no contention over religious leadership, and Riyadh and Tehran managed their relation-

---

[1]   For an Iranian view of relations, see Hamid Hadyan, "Exploring Iran-Saudi Relations in Light of New Regional Conditions," *Rahbord* (Tehran), translated by Open Source Center, IAP20061113336001, 16 May 2006.

[2]   Hassan Hanizadeh, "Iran, Saudi Arabia Open a New Chapter in Regional Cooperation," *Tehran Times*, 14 June 2008.

ship without significant turmoil, particularly after the 1968 announce-ment of the departure of British forces from the Gulf.[3] The tenor of their dealings was nonetheless strained over the issue of regional hier-archy, OPEC leadership, and a multilateral approach to Gulf security. As noted by Shahram Chubin and Charles Tripp, the fundamental obstacle during this period—and one that continues to contribute to today's tribulations—was Saudi Arabia's "unwillingness to be a junior partner in the local system, and its inability to be an equal partner."[4]

The 1979 Revolution in Iran, however, exacerbated these geostrategic differences by injecting into Iran's policy behavior a revo-lutionary ideology that was anti-monarchical, universalist, and anti-imperial. For rulers in Riyadh, the fall of the Shah and the rise of Khomeini was a veritable earthquake, threatening the territorial integ-rity of Saudi Arabia by appealing to its disenfranchised Shi'a population in the Eastern Province, unsettling the al-Saud's confidence about the reliability of support from the United States, challenging their claim to Islamic leadership, and imparting a new vocabulary of resistance to Islamists across the region, regardless of their sectarian hue.[5]

The most palpable manifestation of the new threat inside Saudi Arabia was the siege of the Grand Mosque in Mecca by followers of Juhayman al-Utaybi in 1979, followed shortly thereafter by a Shi'a *intifada* (uprising) in the Eastern Province.[6] Less visibly and more long-

---

[3] For relations during this period, see Faisal bin Salman, *Iran, Saudi Arabia, and the Gulf: Power Politics in Transition,* London: I. B. Tauris, 2003.

[4] Shahram Chubin and Charles Tripp, "Iran-Saudi Arabia Relations and Regional Order," *Adelphi Paper,* Vol. 204, London: International Institute for Strategic Studies, Oxford Uni-versity Press, 1996, p. 9.

[5] For an example of the Revolution's impact on a Sunni Islamist movement, the Egyptian Muslim Brotherhood, see Rudee Mathee, "The Egyptian Opposition on the Iranian Revolu-tion," in Juan R. I. Cole and Nikki R. Keddie, *Shi'ism and Social Protest,* New Haven, Conn.: Yale University Press, 1986. For more background on Saudi perceptions of the Iranian Revo-lution, see David E. Long, "The Impact of the Iranian Revolution on the Arabian Peninsula and the Gulf States," in John L. Esposito, *The Iranian Revolution: Its Global Impact,* Miami: Florida International Press, 1990, pp. 100–115.

[6] For the Shi'a uprising in the Eastern province, see Toby Craig Jones, "Rebellion on the Saudi Periphery: Modernity, Marginalization and the Shia Uprising of 1979," *International Journal of Middle East Studies,* Vol. 38, 2006.

term, the Iranian Revolution placed intense pressure on the al-Saud from their own religious bureaucracy by providing a model of government that accorded primacy to the clerical class and cast a spotlight on the perceived impiety of the Saudi royal family.[7] Among certain members of the al-Saud, the fall of the Shah was also an indirect indictment of recent Saudi reforms under King Faysal, demonstrating the potentially violent response of an Islamicized society that had been subjected to too rapid and too sweeping a modernization.[8]

From the point of view of Saudi Arabia, the Soviet Union's invasion of Afghanistan in 1979 was a godsend: a chance to reaffirm its Islamic legitimacy in the face of challenges by Khomeini, both to international audiences and to domestic constituents.[9] As noted by Vali Nasr in his testimony before the U.S. Senate Foreign Relations Committee, the resulting ideological rivalry between the two states "served as the context for radicalization that ultimately led to 9/11."[10] Aside from subsidizing the recruitment, travel, and training of foreign jihadist volunteers to Afghanistan, Riyadh sponsored the production of an expansive array of anti-Shi'a and anti-Iranian tracts, designed to highlight the narrowly ethnic and sectarian aspirations of the Khomeinist regime and mitigate its more universal appeal throughout the region and the world.[11] As discussed further below, many of these publications have

---

[7]   Madawi al-Rasheed, *Contesting the Saudi State: Islamic Voices from a New Generation,* New York: Cambridge University Press, 2007b, p. 105.

[8]   Chubin and Tripp (1996, pp. 9–10). See also Sa'ad Badib, *Al-'Alaqat al-Saudiya al-Iraniya, 1932–1983 [Saudi-Iranian Relations, 1932–1983],* London: The Center for Iranian-Arab Relations, 1994.

[9]   The invasion also provided a fig leaf to counter Iran's accusation that Saudi support to Iraq was divisive and harmful to larger Islamic causes.

[10]   Quoted in Beehner (2007).

[11]   Madawi al-Rasheed has argued that by challenging the al-Saud's claim to pan-Islamic legitimacy, the Iranian Revolution effectively "universalized" its Salafi discourse, which had thus far promoted jihad within the domestic context of the state's foundation (al-Rasheed, 2007b, p. 105).

enjoyed renewed currency within jihadist and radical Salafi circles today.[12]

For its part, Iran sought to extend its influence both near and far, by offering safe haven and varying degrees of support to dissident Shi'a groups such as the Organization for the Islamic Revolution on the Arabian Peninsula (OIR), the Islamic Front for the Liberation of Bahrain (IFLB), the Hizb-e Wahdat in Afghanistan, the Da'awa Party in Iraq, various Hizballah groups in Kuwait and the Gulf, and of course the Lebanese Hizballah.[13] However, several of the Gulf groups had more local, indigenous roots among Shi'a clerical currents in Kuwait and Iraq rather than in Qom; their philosophical inspiration from the Islamic Revolution did not necessarily entail political obedience to Tehran's ambitions.[14]

The annual Hajj pilgrimage to Mecca provided another highly sensitive and symbolic arena for Tehran to rattle the al-Saud by inciting Iranian pilgrims toward revolutionary activism and rhetoric. Recurring tensions reached their apex in 1987 when over 450 Iranian pilgrims were killed by Saudi security forces, with the result that the two countries totally severed their diplomatic relations for three years.[15] Today,

---

[12] One key example is the renewed popularity of an anti-Khomeinist book written shortly after the Revolution, purportedly by a prominent cleric at the Islamic University of Medina; the tract was quoted extensively by Abu Musab al-Zarqawi in a four-hour diatribe recorded shortly before his death in June 2006. The book is by Mohammad Abdallah al-Gharib, believed by many analysts to be a pseudonym for Mohammad Surur Zayn al-Abidin, an influential Syrian-born cleric at the Islamic University of Medina. See Mohammad Abdallah al-Gharib, *Wa Ja'a Dur al-Majus [And Then Came the Turn of the Magi]*, n.p., 1983; as well as the transcript of the audio recording by Abu Musab al-Zarqawi, "Hal Ataka Hadith al-Rawafidh? [Has Word of the Rejectionists (Shi'as) Reached You?]," n.d.

[13] It should be noted that, during the 1990s, these Gulf-based groups abandoned their violent agenda and instead worked to promote change peaceably. For the transformation of the OIR into the Islah movement, see Foud Ibrahim, *The Shi'is of Saudi Arabia*, London, England: Dar al-Saqi, 2007. The IFLB became the Islamic Action Society (IAS). RAND interviews in al-Qatif, al-Dammam, March 2007, and Manama, November 2006.

[14] For background on the origin of Shi'a dissident movements in Saudi Arabia, Kuwait, and Bahrain and their relationship with Iran, see Laurence Louër, *Transnational Shia Politics: Religious and Political Networks in the Gulf*, London, England: Hurst and Company, 2008.

[15] Chubin and Tripp (1996, p. 17).

some Saudi analysts point to the Hajj as a vulnerable arena for Iranian retaliation against the Kingdom, particularly in the circumstances of a U.S. attack on Iran.[16]

Aside from the Soviet invasion of Afghanistan, the other, more important conflict that profoundly affected Saudi-Iranian relations was Iraq's invasion of Iran in 1980. The status and orientation of Iraq has always been an important determinant of the Gulf geometry of power and especially so for Riyadh and Tehran; *a weak Iraq can arguably be said to increase rivalry between Saudi Arabia and Iran, whereas a strong Iraq can stabilize or moderate the tensions.*[17] Iran viewed the unprovoked attack by Saddam Hussein as having been undertaken partially in the service of Saudi interests to eradicate the Revolution. Saudi Arabia supported Iraq as a buffer against Iran. Yet it was the war's impact on changes in the regional order that further strained relations.

The war provided the context for the massive introduction of U.S. military aid and forces into the region, largely at Riyadh's invitation, which in Tehran's view fatally tipped the local balance of power to its disadvantage. The establishment of U.S. Central Command under the Carter Doctrine, the sale of the Airborne Warning and Control System (AWACS) to Saudi Arabia in 1980–1981, and the creation of the GCC in 1981 were all viewed in Tehran as net gains for Saudi Arabia. In 1984, the effect of American military assistance to Riyadh was palpably felt by Tehran when Saudi aircraft, using U.S.-supplied AWACS information, shot down two Iranian planes that had reportedly violated Saudi airspace.

The Iran-Iraq cease-fire in 1988 apparently vindicated the Saudi policy of using Iraq as a local buffer against Iran, while in Tehran, the war's termination spawned an intense reevaluation of Iranian Gulf policy that became gradually less antagonistic. The death of Khomeini and the subsequent struggle between the more pragmatic president, Ali Akbar Hashemi Rafsanjani, and the Supreme Leader successor, Ali Khamenei, showed how Iran's factionalized political system and dispersed decisionmaking structure can contribute to tension and confu-

---

[16] RAND interviews with Saudi analysts in Jeddah and Riyadh, March 2007.

[17] Chubin and Tripp (1996, p. 39).

sion in the Saudi-Iranian bilateral relationship. At various times since 1979, Riyadh has found it difficult to discern coherence in Iranian policy amidst the cacophony of competing voices.[18]

In both states, the impetus for a gradual warming of relations throughout the 1990s stemmed from a number of domestic and regional factors.[19] Understanding these is important for separating the structural sources of tension that divide the two states from the more fluid and dynamic variables.

The 1990 invasion of Kuwait highlighted Saddam's Iraq as a shared threat to both countries, and Tehran's lack of support to the Shi'a intifada in 1991 in southern Iraq sent the first signal to Riyadh that the era of revolutionary expansion may have ended. The subsequent postwar domestic crisis in Saudi Arabia—marked by unemployment hovering at 12 percent, a concerted Islamist challenge to the royal family due to the stationing of U.S. troops on Saudi soil, and a dispute over succession—strengthened the argument for rapprochement among key segments of the royal family.[20] By the end of 1991 the two countries had restored diplomatic relations with the historic visit of Saudi Foreign Minister Saud al-Faysal to Tehran.

It is important to note, however, that despite the increasingly high levels of diplomatic meetings and joint communications that characterized the early 1990s, fundamental tensions between the two states continued to be played out in a number of important theaters. Most notably, the collapse of the Soviet Union and the emergence of the new republics in the Caucasus and Central Asia created a new zone

---

[18] Chubin and Tripp (1996, p. 19).

[19] Gawdat Bahgat, "Iranian-Saudi Rapprochement. Prospects and Implications," *World Affairs*, Vol. 162, No. 3, Winter 2000; Gwen Okruhlik, "Saudi Arabian-Iranian Relations: External Rapprochement and Internal Consolidation," *Middle East Policy*, Vol. 10, No. 2, Summer 2003. Iranian commentators have more recently maintained that the tensions all along were the result of either Ba'athist propaganda or U.S. instigation. For example, a *Tehran Times* columnist in 2006 wrote that "foreign powers that were concerned about the establishment of solidarity among countries on the north and south of the Persian Gulf attempted to create division between Iran and members of the Persian Gulf Cooperation Council" (Hanizadeh, 2008).

[20] Okruhlik (2003, p. 117).

of political, economic, and cultural contestation. Aside from ensuring that the independence of these states did not inspire similar breakaway impulses among its own ethnic populations, Tehran was keen to expand its influence in Central Asia as compensation for the influence it had lost in the Gulf.[21]

For its part, Saudi Arabia indirectly supported the United States' efforts to counter Iranian influence by backing Turkey's appeal to pan-Turkism in the region. But Riyadh also saw the area as ripe for the spread of Salafism among the predominately Sunni populations of the Central Asian republics as a means to "out-Islamicize" Tehran's similar efforts.[22] Tajikistan offers an illustrative example of how Saudi Arabia effectively bested Iran's efforts; Tajiks proved largely tone-deaf to Iran's zealous promotion of their shared Persian heritage and language ties, while Riyadh's massive investment in religious infrastructure and media met with a more receptive audience.[23] For Saudi Arabia, the Tajik episode demonstrated an important feature of future bilateral contention with Tehran—the importance of simply outspending the Iranians in the cultural and media sphere.

Afghanistan after the withdrawal of Soviet troops was another contested arena; Iran and its allied Hazara groups were sidelined from Saudi- and U.S.-sponsored Afghan power-sharing accords in 1992 and 1993.[24] Iran was also surprisingly slow to appreciate the threat from the Saudi-backed Taliban, and it was only after the fall of Kabul in 1996 and Mazar-e Sharif in 1998 that Iranian aid to the anti-Taliban alliance gathered steam.[25]

Aside from Central Asia, tensions continued to play out elsewhere on the Arabian Peninsula during the early 1990s. Much of this stemmed

---

[21] Henner Furtig, *Iran's Rivalry with Saudi Arabia Between the Gulf Wars,* New York: Ithaca Press, 2006, p. 179.

[22] Furtig (2006, p. 195).

[23] Furtig (2006, p. 204).

[24] Ahmed Rashid, *Taliban: Militant Islam, Oil and Fundamentalism in Central Asia,* New Haven, Conn.: Yale University Press, 2000, p. 199. See also Mohsen Milani, "Iran's Policy Toward Afghanistan," *Middle East Journal,* Vol. 60, No. 2, Spring 2006.

[25] Rashid (2000, p. 203).

from Tehran's increasing concern about the presence of U.S. forces in the region as a barrier to a more localized security and economic system in which Iran would be the dominant player.[26] During a 1992 border incident between Qatar and Saudi Arabia, Iran evinced open support for Qatar's position and offered the tiny kingdom a defense treaty and a supply of 30,000 troops.[27] In 1994, Iran lambasted Saudi Arabia's support for secessionist south Yemen during the Yemeni civil war as an oblique attack on the GCC policy more generally, which has traditionally sought to weaken Yemen. In 1996, Bahrain's al-Khalifa government, longtime clients of the al-Saud, announced the capture of coup plotters who had reportedly been trained by the Lebanese Hizballah and Iran's Islamic Revolutionary Guards Corps (IRGC). The same year also saw the bombing of the U.S. Air Force barracks at Khobar Towers in Dharan, Saudi Arabia, purportedly by members of an Iranian-trained Saudi Hizballah cell.[28] None of these provocations actually advanced Iran's position, but rather caused increased confusion and suspicion in Riyadh.[29]

The ascendancy of Crown Prince Abdullah in 1995 gave the push toward détente new momentum. Abdullah enjoyed comparatively greater legitimacy among domestic Islamists than his predecessor, King Fahd, and thus felt more empowered to pursue regional initiatives. He reportedly saw value in bolstering Rafsanjani's pragmatic outreach, fearing that Iran could fall back to the hardliners if the new

---

[26] Ray Takeyh, *Hidden Iran: Paradox and Power in the Islamic Republic,* New York: Times Books, 2007, p. 68.

[27] Chubin and Tripp (1996, p. 36).

[28] This is a subject of some debate: For example, the bombing has also been linked to al-Qaeda. For a persuasive argument refuting al-Qaeda's involvement, see Thomas Hegghamer, "Deconstructing the Myth About al-Qa'ida and Khobar," *CTC Sentinel,* Vol. 1, No. 3, February 2008, pp. 20–22.

[29] For a time line of Saudi-Iran relations, see Furtig (2006, pp. 249–263). At the level of ideology and media, Iran continued in the early 1990s to promote anti-Saud propaganda. An illustrative example is the journal *Risalaat al-Haramayn,* published from 1991 to 1995 in Beirut under Iranian sponsorship and affiliated with the Saudi Hizballah. The periodical played to a Saudi Shi'a audience, but also tried to exploit regional Hijazi resentment toward the Najd. See Ibrahim (2007, p. 195).

president were not supported. This prerogative culminated in a historic meeting between the two leaders on the sidelines of the Organization of the Islamic Conference (OIC) in Pakistan in 1997. There, Abdullah reportedly assured Iran that the presence of U.S. troops in the region to contain Iran was inadvisable in the long term and gave his unequivocal support to Iran's presidency in the OIC. In return, Rafsanjani agreed to ensure that Iranian pilgrims would not incite disturbances during the Hajj.[30] Finally, Saudi Arabia's refusal to implicate Iran as the state sponsor for the bombing of the U.S. Air Force barracks at Khobar Towers has been interpreted by some observers as an additional gesture of goodwill; as recently as 2007, Saudi diplomats told RAND researchers that Iran "owes" Riyadh for this gesture.[31]

The latter half of the 1990s, particularly under the "Good Neighbor" policy of Iranian President Mohammed Khatami, saw a strengthening of the groundwork for détente that Rafsanjani had laid, but with a significant shift in tone. Khatami's breakthrough policy was to effectively "compartmentalize" Iran's insistence on the departure of U.S. forces from the region from its efforts to build good relations with the Gulf states, despite their dependence on American support.[32] Defense Minister Vice Admiral Ali Shamkhani, himself an ethnic Arab, emerged as the new administration's principal point man for this charm offensive; his fluency in Arabic reportedly served to reinforce Tehran's commitment to improving relations and helped build personal rapport with a number of Gulf leaders.[33] The warming culminated in the historic visit of the Iranian president to Jeddah in 1999, followed by a number of regional and security agreements in 2001 and

---

[30] Keynoush (2007, p. 157).

[31] RAND interview with Saudi diplomats in Riyadh, March 2007.

[32] Takeyh (2007, p. 68).

[33] Mohsen Milani, "Iran's Gulf Policy: From Idealism and Confrontation to Pragmatism and Moderation," in Jamal S. al-Suwaidi, *Iran and the Gulf: A Search for Stability,* Abu Dhabi: Emirates Center for Strategic Studies and Research, 1996; Kenneth R. Timmerman, "The Saudi-Iranian Thaw," *The Wall Street Journal,* 26 May 1999; Howard Schneider, "Saudi Pact with Iran is Sign of Growing Trust," *The Washington Post,* 17 April 2001; Douglas Jehl "On Trip to Mend Ties, Iran's President Meets Saudi Prince," *The New York Times,* 17 May 1999.

2002 covering terrorism, money laundering, drug trafficking, and illegal immigration.

Following September 11th and the collapse of the Taliban, the two states increasingly coordinated on countering al-Qaeda. In the months preceding the U.S. invasion of Iraq, Riyadh and Tehran issued joint declarations opposing any U.S. invasion, fearing a potential spillover of post-Saddam disintegration.[34] But Iraq's subsequent descent into internal strife, the influx of foreign fighters, the political ascendancy of Iran's Shi'a allies, and Tehran's growing influence more broadly all conspired to overturn the previous push for rapprochement.

The election of President Ahmadinejad in 2005 accelerated this trend by imparting a triumphalist, nationalistic, and excessively strident tone to Iranian policy, which contrasted sharply with the conciliatory efforts of the Khatami administration. This shift in tone provides the backdrop for understanding the current dynamics that shape relations between the two countries.

Iran's "Arab Street" Strategy Provokes Dissent Inside Saudi Arabia

Speaking to RAND researchers at a roundtable meeting in 2007, a Saudi scholar noted that, were it not for Iran's incitement, "Sunnis and Shi'as in the Middle East would live as brothers." "Sectarianism is a major part of Iran's foreign policy," noted another observer.[35] Yet the record of Iranian and Saudi behavior since the fall of Saddam suggests just the opposite.

Since the invasion of Iraq and in particular since the election of Ahmadinejad, Iran has pursued what can best be described as an aggressively *nonsectarian*, "Arab street" strategy that appeals to Arab publics by emphasizing Iran's commitment to the Palestinian cause, opposition to Western imperialism in the region, and resistance to U.S.

---

[34] Keynoush (2007, pp. 183–193).

[35] RAND discussion with Saudi foreign ministry officials, Riyadh, March 2007.

pressure on the nuclear issue.[36] As noted by an official in the Lebanese Hizballah's research wing,

> At the heart of Iran's foreign policy are two key issues: the Palestinian cause and confronting Washington's hegemonic schemes in the region. There is nothing particularly Shia about the two issues. Indeed, both have been presented as causes for the majority of Sunni Arabs. *In this sense, Iran's foreign policy is Sunni* (italics added).[37]

Popular Saudi columnist Mshari al-Dhaydi appeared to echo this interpretation, urging his readers in *al-Sharq al-Awsat* in July 2007, to

> examine all the big Arab portfolios—Lebanon, Palestine, and Iraq. They are being stolen from Arab hands ... and turned over to Iranian hands gradually.[38]

Yet Iran's hyperactivism on pan-Arab issues is not necessarily proof of its influence, but rather just the opposite—an effort to overcompensate for its fundamental isolation from the rest of region. Despite its claims to universalism, it remains the odd man out.[39] By its own admission, it has largely failed in its attempt to refashion the

---

[36] It is important to note that internally, President Ahmadinejad aggressively promoted aspects of Shi'a theology, particularly the concept of the *Mahdaviat* or return of the Hidden Twelfth Imam. This messianic posturing, along with Iran's nuclear ambitions, certainly rattled Saudi Arabia and the Gulf, but it was not an explicitly sectarian strategy that tried to denigrate Sunnis. Indeed, Iran's official pronouncements have tended to emphasize that the Taliban, al-Qaeda, and anti-Shi'a *takfiris* are aberrations from Islam. For more on the role of apocalyptic thought in Iran's policy calculations under Ahmadinejad, see Mehdi Khalaji, "Apocalyptic Politics: On the Rationality of Iranian Policy," *Policy Focus*, No. 79, Washington, D.C.: Washington Institute for Near East Policy, 2008.

[37] Hizballah think tank official Ali Fayyad, quoted in Abd al-Latif (2007).

[38] Mshari al-Dhaydi, "Uhadhir an Taqdhi Alihi al-Ama'im [I Warn the Religious Establishment]," *al-Sharq al-Awsat*, 19 July 2007.

[39] Joost Hiltermann has noted, "[Iran] wants to have the greatest influence possible, and it can only do that if it is not a sectarian actor ... It can be more effective if it does not play the Shi'a card." Quoted in Scott Peterson, "Saudi Arabia, Iran Target Mideast's Sectarian Discord," *Christian Science Monitor*, 5 March 2007.

Arab world in its image, reflected most visibly by the fact that Gulf Shi'a groups that received Iranian endorsement (the Islamic Front for the Liberation of Bahrain, the Organization for the Islamic Revolution on the Arabian Peninsula, and the Supreme Council for the Islamic Revolution in Iraq) have all distanced themselves from their erstwhile patron and its revolutionary ideals, through name changes or a more substantial reorientation of goals.

Nonetheless, Iran's belief, whether warranted or not, that it can draw support from Arab publics has impelled Tehran toward brinkmanship and bravado in its policy toward Saudi Arabia. This is nowhere as evident as on the Israeli-Palestinian issue.

The Israeli-Palestinian Issue Is a Key Component of Iran's "Arab Street" Strategy

In the Saudi-Iran relationship, the Israeli-Palestinian issue appears to have acquired significant ideological sensitivity. Supreme Leader Khamenei termed Palestine as "a limb of our body" at the height of the Palestinian *intifada* in 2000.[40] Iran matches its rhetoric with increasing financial support to Hamas and the Palestinian Islamic Jihad (PIJ), making it such a major player in Gaza that an Egyptian ex–foreign ministry official lamented to RAND in 2008, "The Iranians used to come to us and talk about Palestine and we would say, 'who . . . are you to tell us about Palestine.' Now when they come, we *have* to listen."[41]

The seizure of pan-Arab issues by Iran has thus inspired alarm, but also a degree of jealousy in Riyadh, which has long prided itself on Arab leadership on the Israeli-Palestinian issue—especially in light of Egypt's retreat from the regional stage since the Camp David Accords. Saudi officials appear particularly incensed that Iran can win over Palestinian loyalties, and especially loyalty from Hamas, while Riyadh's mediation efforts have been fruitless.[42]

---

[40] Shaul Shai, *The Axis of Evil: Iran, Hizballah, and the Palestinian Terror*, Piscataway, N.J.: Transaction Books, 2005, p. 149.

[41] RAND discussion with ex-Egyptian foreign ministry official, Cairo, Egypt, March 2008.

[42] See Karen Elliot House, "Saudi Balancing Act," *The Wall Street Journal*, 4 April 2007.

Rhetorically, Iranian officials have presented themselves as paragons of virtue on the Israeli-Palestinian issue, often with the calculated intent of embarrassing Saudi Arabia. An example of this dynamic was Ahmadinejad's speech denying the Holocaust in the presence of King Abdullah at a 2005 summit in Mecca. The Iranian president's remarks were a brazen act of one-upsmanship that left the al-Saud mortified and unable to respond.[43] There continues to be disdain for Iran's involvement in Palestinian affairs, with Saudi diplomats telling RAND researchers in March 2007 that this "is an Arab issue, so why is Iran involved?"[44]

Iran's Support for Hizballah in 2006 Was a Turning Point

It was the actions of Iran's principal Levantine ally, Hizballah, during the summer 2006 that presented the most powerful pan-Arab trump card to the al-Saud. A Shi'a organization backed by Saudi Arabia's strategic rival had effectively bested the vaunted Israeli Defense Forces, galvanizing Arab opinion and undercutting Sunni Arab regimes who had long evinced opposition to Israel, but with little to show for it. The debate over whether to lend moral and rhetorical support to Hizballah exposed the fundamental paradox between the al-Saud's broader aspirations to pan-Arab leadership and the more insular doctrinal aversion to Shiism of its Salafi clerical establishment.

It is critical to emphasize that, like the 1979 Revolution, the event was "read" by various domestic actors in Saudi Arabia through different lenses: Those with a more vested interest in the system and the rule of the al-Saud decried Hizballah for provoking an Israeli attack, sowing *fitna* (discord), and pursuing narrowly sectarian goals. Those farther out from the Saudi circle of power, particularly semi-official clerics from the Sahwa or "awakened" current, seized upon the war to highlight the caution, immobility, impiety, and—in some cases— illegitimacy of the Saudi regime.[45] Even farther from the Salafi center,

---

[43] See Girard (2005).

[44] RAND interviews in Riyadh, March 2007.

[45] "Saudi Daily Views Heated Debate Between Clerics on Shi'a Threat, Hizballah," *al-Watan* (Abha), translated by Open Source Center, GMP2006092814005, 28 September 2006.

there were sporadic demonstrations by Shi'a communities in the Eastern Province in solidarity with Hizballah and, indirectly, with Iran. Yet these were likely motivated by the same sentiment that spawned similar demonstrations in Cairo, Amman, and elsewhere—applause for Hizballah and Iran for challenging Israel and shaking up the stagnant political order, rather than any expressions of sectarian affinity.

Regardless of whether they demonstrated, Shi'as in the Eastern Province of Saudi Arabia during this period were subjected to growing pressures, both from the regime, which feared them as a potential fifth column for Iran, and from hard-line Salafi clerics, whose anti-Shi'a pronouncements against Hizballah had a reverberating "echo effect" on these communities. As will be discussed at length in the next section, our discussions in the Eastern Province in March 2007 revealed the lingering effect of the war: increased harassment by Salafi hardliners from the Najd, arrests, censorship, and the restriction of cultural and religious freedoms. Taken in sum, the war placed incredible stress on the Saudi regime, exposing fissures and tensions from multiple quarters.

Irrespective of whether the summer 2006 war was launched at Iran's suggestion, Tehran emerged from the conflict with the upper hand in the bilateral relationship—at least in terms of Arab public opinion.[46] From Qom and Mashhad, Iranian clerics attacked Saudi Arabia's official clerics (derided as "court *ulema*") as being increasingly out of touch with the sentiment of the Saudi populace and Arab pub-

---

[46] A 2006 Zogby/University of Maryland poll following the 2006 Lebanon war asked 3,850 respondents in Egypt, Jordan, Lebanon, Morocco, Saudi Arabia, and the United Arab Emirates to identify the two countries who posed the greatest threat to their security; only 11 percent identified Iran, contrasted with 85 percent who listed Israel and 72 percent who cited the United States. Among world leaders most admired by respondents, Hizballah leader Hasan Nasrallah came in first, while Ahmadinejad came in third, after French president Jacques Chirac (Zogby International, 2006). A separate poll by *al-Arabiya* in February 2007 revealed similar unease, extending to Iran's ambitions throughout the Arab world. See *Al-Arabiya*, "Banorama: Kayf Yanthur al-Arab Iran? [Panorama: How Do Arabs View Iran?]," 26 February 2007. Domestically, however, the Arab trump card may have come at a price; there was anecdotal reporting of popular dissent inside Iran against the regime's lavish support to Hizballah, especially given the dire state of the Iranian economy. See Azadeh Moaveni, "Why Iran Isn't Cheering," *Time*, 23 July 2006.

lics, who were largely supportive of Hizballah.[47] In postwar polling in Egypt, Ahmadinejad came in second after Nasrallah as the most important leader in the region. From Saudi Arabia's perspective, a particularly galling aspect of the war was a reported spike in Sunni conversions to Shiism in Syria, Egypt, and even in the Sudan.[48] Here again, the phenomena was less an expression of sectarian affinity and more a signal of *political* solidarity with the "winning sect," which seemed to be ascendant in Iraq and was the only regional power capable of challenging Israel. The trend appears to have grown worrisome enough that King Abdullah took the rare step of issuing a public warning that regionwide efforts at Shi'a proselytizing would fail.[49] Although not named, Iran's support was implied.

Through the actions of its Lebanese ally Hizballah, Iran prompted a barrage of anti-Shi'a invective by the Saudi clerical establishment as a rearguard action against the "regime-versus-public" fissures that the Hizballah war had exposed. This sectarian offensive by Saudi voices intensified in the wake of subsequent U.S. deliberations about a withdrawal from Iraq. The vocabulary and parameters of this discourse—as well as its local effect on the status of Gulf Shi'as and, more broadly, bilateral relations between Saudi Arabia and Iran—will be covered next.

Anti-Shiism in Saudi Arabia: Manifestations and Effects

As noted earlier, the 1980s saw a flurry of anti-Shi'a publications by the Saudi clerical establishment designed to blunt the ideological appeal of the Iranian Revolution.[50] Many of these texts today have been resur-

---

[47] Middle East Media Research Institute, "An Eternal Curse on the Muftis of the Saudi Court and on the Pharaoh of Egypt," *Jomhouri-ye Eslami*, 28 July 2006.

[48] Ellen Knickmeyer, "In Syria, Converting for Sake of Politics: Hezbollah's Gains During Lebanon War Inspire Sunnis to Become Shiis," *The Washington Post*, 6 October 2006.

[49] Interview with King Abdullah, *al-Siyasa* (Kuwait) January 27, 2007.

[50] For historical overviews, see Hamid Algar, *Wahhabism: A Critical Essay,* North Haledon, N.J.: Islamic Publications International, 2002; Hala Fattah, "'Wahhabi' Influences, Salafi

rected and enjoy a newfound resonance among certain Sunni audiences in the context of the fall of Saddam Hussein and the growing perception of Shi'a ascendancy across the region.

It is important first to characterize the extent of the Saudi regime's official relationship to anti-Shi'a discourse. Several analysts have described the policy as one of willful neglect or tacit endorsement, but not necessarily explicit promotion.[51] Official Saudi voices emphasize that it is Iran's policy behavior and regional ambitions, not Shiism per se, that fuels their concern. Domestically, King Abdullah starting in 2003 held a series of well-publicized and high-level National Dialogue sessions that focused on recognizing and bridging the gap with the internal "other"—fostering dialogue among Sufis, Salafis, Shi'as, and other sects within Saudi Arabia. For a state that has traditionally eschewed any acknowledgement of internal religious plurality, this was a remarkable development.

Yet in discussions with RAND researchers, Saudi reformists and Shi'a clerics suggested that the National Dialogue sessions had no effect on the Salafi establishment; one reformer termed the meetings "hollow debating societies."[52] By the end of 2006, the regime was doing little to rescind or counter the anti-Shi'a *fatawa* that were being issued by popular Salafi clerics. The shrillest and most damaging of these occurred at the height of Saudi uncertainty about a U.S. withdrawal from Iraq and fears of Iran potentially filling the power vacuum.

In the official Saudi press, there was widespread speculation about a secret deal between the United States and Iran, and Prince Turki al-

---

Responses: Shaikh Mahmud Shukri and the Iraqi Salafi Movement, 1745–1930," *Journal of Islamic Studies,* Vol. 14, No. 2, 2003, pp. 127–148; and Mohammad Rasul, *Al-Wahhabiyyun wa al-'Iraq [The Wahhabis and Iraq],* Beirut: Riad el-Rayyes Books, 2005.

[51] Jones (2007) has written, "Unlike in the 1980s, when Saudi Arabia met the ideological threat posed by Khomeini head-on, the kingdom's rulers have not consistently manipulated sectarian hostility." Yet he later concludes that "managing and strategically deploying anti-Shiism is nevertheless an important part of [King Abdullah]'s government's political calculus." Gause (2007a) has argued for a similar ambivalence in Saudi policy, noting that "the Saudi government itself has not played the sectarian card in recent crises" but still frames it as a form of "cynical manipulation" and likens it to "playing with fire."

[52] RAND interview with a Sunni reformist, Jeddah, March 2007.

Faysal publicly warned the United States not to withdraw. In October 2006, Saudi officials met with Harith al-Dhari, leader of the Association of Muslim Scholars, potentially signaling their drift toward a more activist role.[53] On December 10, 38 Saudi clerics joined Iraqi clerics in signing a statement denouncing the killing and displacement of Iraqi Sunnis at the hands of Shi'as and said, "we should openly side with our Sunni brothers in Iraq and lend them all appropriate forms of support." The signatories included noted Sahwa shaykhs Safar bin Abd al-Rahman al-Hawali and Nasr al-Umar.[54] Other clerics soon followed suit.[55]

All of this occurred in a more generalized climate of anti-Iranian seething that followed the execution of Saddam Hussein, which, because of its occurrence on the last night of Ramadan and the taunting of the ex-president by prison guards allied with Muqtada al-Sadr, was characterized in many Arab press outlets as having been orchestrated by Iran with U.S. connivance.[56] In Iran, the *fatawa* elicited a firm rebuke from clerics and officials.

In the context of growing tensions with Iran over Iraq, particularly since 2006, Saudi Arabia's anti-Shi'a rhetoric can be considered partly a calculated *political action* rather than solely a symptom of a deeper sectarian divide between the two states. Faced with pressure

---

[53] Abdullah Shihri, "Clerics Urge Muslims to Back Iraq Sunnis," Associated Press, 12 December 2006.

[54] The text of the *fatwa* is available at the Web site of Saudi cleric Nasr al-Umar (Nasr al-Umar, homepage, no date).

[55] For others, see "Shaykh Salman al-Awda Warns of Sectarian War in Iraq, Holds the US Responsible," *Islam Today*, translated by Open Source Center, GMP20061107866002, 5 November 2006.

[56] Gause (2007a). The Saddam execution and Iran's conduct in Iraq more generally have the effect of negating whatever goodwill and support it has engendered in Arab opinion because of its support to Palestinian groups and Hizballah. Less than six months after the July 2006 war, available polling and media surveys revealed a noticeable drop in Arab public support for Iran—stemming principally from worsening sectarian violence in Iraq. *Zogby's* February–March 2007 survey showed that a majority of respondents believed Iran's role in Iraq was unhelpful. In an interview with RAND in Amman in February 2008, a Jordanian analyst noted that there were "two Irans" in Arab opinion: a good one (for supporting Palestinians) and a bad one (for perpetuating crimes against Iraq's Sunnis).

from their clerical establishment, yet cognizant of anti-Shiism's mobilizing potential, Saudi leaders released the pressure valve on this ideology at a critical juncture.

Saudi-Iranian Tensions Have Slowed Pro-Shi'a Reforms

This strategy, however, had little deterrent effect on Iran or its Shi'a allies. The real impact was felt among Saudi Arabia's own Shi'as and their efforts to secure increased civil and political liberties. In the Eastern Province, our interviews suggest that the deterioration of Saudi-Iranian relations and the resulting anti-Shi'a vitriol from Salafi clerics were having a chilling effect on the regime's previous reforms toward its Shi'a citizens. Some of our interlocutors framed the problem as one of willful negligence; despite King Abdullah's overtures to the Shi'as at a *national* level, the regime has consistently pursued what one interviewee termed a "shut-eye policy" on anti-Shi'a abuse at the *local* level—tolerating or not cracking down sufficiently on instances of discrimination.[57] The official channels for reform were increasingly seen as a ploy to keep the Shi'as engaged and "talking," rather than "acting."

Another important by-product of Saudi-Iran tensions has been the fraying of reform cooperation among Sunni and Shi'a activists inside Saudi Arabia. In discussions with RAND researchers, Sunni liberals in Jeddah pointed to growing distrust between Sunni reformists and their Shi'a counterparts in the Eastern Province. Much of this is due to the "echo effect" of the wars in Lebanon and Iraq: Saudi Sunnis interpret Shi'a support for Sadr and Hizballah as an expression of a "winner take all" mentality that allows no cooperation across sectarian lines. For their part, Shi'a reformists believe that some of their Sunni allies are "closet Wahhabis."

---

[57] Frederic M. Wehrey, "Saudi Arabia: Shi'a Pessimistic on Reform, But Seek Reconciliation," Carnegie Endowment for International Peace, *Arab Reform Bulletin,* June 2007; "Saudi Authorities Close Down Shi'ite Mosque in al-Ihsa Governorate" (al-Rasid report by Mohammad Ali in al-Munayzilah headed: "Security authorities close mosque in village of al-Munayzilah"), translated by Open Source Center, GMP20061003866002, 2 October 2006; "Saudi Arabia: Report on Arrests in Eastern Region for Sympathizing with Hizballah" (Unattributed report from Qatif: "In al-Qatif, a number of sons of the region arrested), translated by Open Source Center, GMP2006101866001, 15 October 2006.

Saudi-Iranian tensions have also highlighted the issue of whether Saudi Shi'as are loyal to the Kingdom or to external *maraja' al-taqlid*—literally, "sources of emulation" (singular, *marja' al-taqlid*)—venerated senior clerics who exert influence over Shi'a social, cultural and, particularly in the case of Iran, political affairs. Since these figures reside in Iran, Iraq, and Lebanon, the institution has fueled Saudi Salafi accusations that the Shi'as are acting as a fifth column for Iran. Our interviews suggest that the most popular of these figures by far is Grand Ayatollah Ali al-Sistani, based in Najaf; according to some interlocutors, 70–80 percent of Saudi Shi'as follow his guidance. Yet during discussions with RAND researchers, Shi'a contacts downplayed al-Sistani's role in Saudi affairs, emphasizing their loyalty to the royal family. Moreover, our interlocutors asserted that other major *maraja'*, such as Sayyid Mohammed Hussein Fadlallah and Ayatollah Mohammed Hadi al-Mudarassi, are careful to avoid speaking specifically about Saudi Shi'a affairs; instead, they restrict their pronouncements to the Shi'as as a whole, to avoid giving the impression of meddling in Saudi Arabia's domestic politics.[58]

Seeking to bolster their nationalist bona fides, some Shi'a intellectuals have pushed for a Saudi-based *hawza* (seminary) for training Shi'a clerics, especially for creating an indigenous, Saudi *marja'*—what one contact referred to as an *ibn al-mintaqa* or "son of the region." In their view, this would expedite the national integration of Shi'as and remove any basis for accusing them of loyalty to foreign authority.[59] It should be noted, however, that this initiative does not enjoy universal support among Shi'a activists; more secular, leftist figures argue that reducing the power of the *maraja'* should itself be a first step in reforming the sect of Shiism, before any national integration can be accomplished.

---

[58] For more on the issue of political involvement by external *marja'*, see Shaykh Hassan al-Saffar, "La wa Lan Nuqbil Aya' Marja'n Takfiri'an wa Arfad Tadkhal aya' Marja' fi al-Shu'un al-Siyasiya al-Dakhiliya li-Biladna [We Do Not and I Will Not Welcome Any *Marja'* (Spiritual Reference) That Promotes *Takfir* (Excommunication) and I Oppose the Interference of Any *Marja'* in the Internal Political Affairs of Our Country]," *al-Risala*, 16 February 2007.

[59] RAND interviews with Shi'a activists in Qatif, March 2007. See also, Saud Salah al-Sarhan, "Nahwa Marja'iyya Shi'a Mustaqlila fi al-Khalij [Toward an Independent Shi'a Source of Emulation]," *al-Sharq al-Awsat*, 24 February 2003.

One of these critics is the Shi'a intellectual Tawfiq al-Sayf, whose book *Nathiriyyat al-Sulta fi Fiqh al-Shi'i [Theories of Political Power in Shi'a Jurisprudence]* criticizes the politicization of the Shi'a clergy, singling out Iran's *vilayet-e faqih* (rule of the supreme jurisconsult; the ideological foundation of the Iranian regime) for special attention.[60]

Despite these explicit intellectual attacks on Iranian ideology, our interviews with Saudi Shi'as did reveal a degree of empathy for Iran. Yet these sentiments are best characterized as spiritual and emotional affinity for Iran as a Shi'a state, rather than admiration for its political ideology or regime. Many acknowledged the dire state of the Iranian economy and the authoritarian character of the regime. One Shi'a contact argued that the Saudi regime's decision to allow Saudi Shi'as to travel to Iran was a master stroke of genius, effectively deflating any possible utopian reverence for Iran. Many Shi'as who went returned with a new appreciation for Saudi Arabia, despite its flaws.

Moreover, some Saudi Shi'a writers and activists have emerged as major voices of anti-Iranian, anti-Khomeinist scholarship, whose resonance extends well beyond the Arabian Peninsula. The aforementioned Tawfiq al-Sayf is one prominent example; aside from his own scholarship, he authored a translation of the work of a major Iranian-born cleric, Shaykh Mohammed Hussein Na'ini.[61] Na'ini's book *Tanbih al-umma wa-tanzih al-milla [Admonishing the Community of Believers and Cleansing the Sect]* critiques the Shi'a precept of waiting for the Hidden Imam, which underpins the legitimacy of clerical rule in Iran. Al-Sayf believes it has also hindered Shi'a efforts at national integration in Saudi Arabia.

Political supporters of Iran in the predominately Shi'a Eastern Province have not fared well. There are reportedly pockets of Iranian sympathy in Qatif, Dammam, Awamiyya, and Safwa. A key pro-Iranian cleric, Hassan al-Nimr, appears to have shed his previous affiliation with Saudi Hizballah and is focused on political activism and sectar-

---

[60] Shaykh Tawfiq al-Sayf, *Nathiriyat al-Sulta fi al-Fiqh al-Shi'i [Theories of Political Power in Shiite Jurisprudence]*, Beirut: Center for Arabic Culture, 2002.

[61] Based in Najaf, Mohammad Hussein Na'ini (1860–1936) taught Ayatollah Abu'l-Qassim Khu'i, who was the mentor of Grand Ayatollah Ali Sistani.

ian reconciliation. In a meeting with RAND researchers, he remained an unapologetic defender of *vilayet-e faqih*, arguing that even Sunni clerics have endorsed this idea, albeit under a different name. Yet in the 2005 municipal council elections, al-Nimr's faction failed to gain a single seat.

Fifth Column Fears Exist at an Unofficial Level, but Are Overblown

As noted earlier, the Iranian Revolution injected a more political dimension to anti-Shi'a Salafi doctrine by raising the specter of Saudi and Gulf Shi'as acting in the service of Tehran. Today, fears of Iran and uncertainty over the future power structure in Iraq have inspired similar distrust of Saudi Shi'as, if not by the Saudi regime then by voices in the militant Salafi milieu. An important marker in the rising preeminence of anti-Shiism as a feature of radical Salafi discourse is the proliferation of Salafi Web sites explicitly devoted to anti-Shiism. Many frequently cite anti-Shi'a rhetoric drawn from the pantheon of Wahhabi-Salafi ideologues, including Mohammed Ibn Abd al-Wahhab, Ibn Taymiyya, Abd al-Aziz Bin Baz, Mohammad Surur Zayn al-Abidin, and Abu Mohammad al-Maqdisi. Aside from theological sources, material on the Web sites is often drawn from Western and Arab press as well as Western think-tank publications translated into Arabic. In these sites and chat rooms, Salafi writers—including such luminaries as the Syrian cleric Abu Basir al-Tartusi and Saudi Arabia's most vitriolic opponent of the Shi'as, Nasr al-'Umar—as well as anonymous chat room posters have envisioned a geography of sectarian conflict that includes not just Saudi Arabia but the entire Middle East, where embattled enclaves of Sunnis confront a growing Shi'a-Iranian menace.[62]

Aside from fearing Shi'a mobilization in the Eastern Province, some Saudi observers believe that Iran could exploit other internal fissures. Saudi Arabia is complex mosaic of local and sectarian identities, bound together by a homogenizing narrative of monarchical state formation that, since the 1920s, has been imposed by force, tribal intermarriage, oil subsidies, school curricula, national celebrations, and

---

[62] Major anti-Shi'a Salafi Web sites include albainah.net, wylsh.com, and khomainy.com.

other cultural practices. Much of this narrative accords primacy to the Najdi heartland, to the detriment of other local and provincial identities.[63] In our interviews in Jeddah and in the east, reformists and activists emphasized this regional hegemony by the center by coining the Arabic term *tanjīd* (literally, "to make something Najdi").[64]

With the fear of internecine strife in Iraq and the rise of Iran, the solidity of this state-building narrative has been subjected to some scrutiny and doubt. Web sites advancing the autonomy of the eastern provinces of Qatif and al-Ahsa, as well as the southwest area of Asir, have recently appeared.[65] Speaking with RAND researchers in March 2007, Saudi analysts in Jedda and Riyadh warned that Iran could seek to exploit these internal fissures by promoting an increased sense of local identity through its transnational media outlets.[66]

Yet overall, the threat of Saudi Shi'as being used as retaliatory agents by Tehran appears overblown. Our Saudi Shi'a contacts, as well as government security sources in Riyadh and Jeddah, do not expect widespread protests, only limited acts of sabotage if the United States were to attack Iran over its alleged nuclear weapons program. First and foremost, Saudi Shi'as remember the aftermath of the 1979 Shi'a uprising in Qatif, which resulted in a severe curtailment of civic freedoms and the virtual militarization of the Eastern Province. They are therefore fearful of taking any actions that could give the regime a pretext for rolling back freedoms they have secured over the past two

---

[63] For more on this construction of national identity, see *al-Jazeera*, "al-Kharita al-Madhhabiya fi al-Sa'udiya [The Sectarian Map in Saudi Arabia]," 6 June 2003; al-Rasheed (2007b). Aside from Saudi Arabia's Eastern Province Shi'as, who are mostly Twelver (Ithna'Ashar) Shi'as, there are Shi'as in Medina (the so-called Nakhawala) and also in the southern province of Najran (the Isma'ilis).

[64] RAND interviews in Jeddah and Qatif, Saudi Arabia, March 2007. For an argument emphasizing the Kingdom as more homogenous in identity—especially in light of the chaos of the Iraq war—see Bernard Haykel's post to the "Middle East Strategy at Harvard" blog ("Saudis United," blog post, Middle East Strategy at Harvard, 16 December 2007).

[65] See the Web site, Dawlat al-Ahsa wa al-Qatif (homepage, no date), which appears to promote militancy and regional autonomy for the eastern region, even arguing for union with Basra. Similarly, the Web site of the "Free State of Asir" has argued for secession of the southwest province, albeit in a peaceful manner (Free State of Asir, homepage, no date).

[66] RAND interviews in Jeddah and Riyadh with Saudi activists and analysts, March 2007.

decades (even if these liberties are incomplete). Others pointed to the extensive Saudi intelligence penetration of the Eastern Province and Sunni villages interspersed among Shi'as as mitigating any serious disruptions.[67]

Iran Also Fears Saudi Incitement of Its Minorities

Perhaps to a greater extent than Saudi Arabia, Iran also fears internal fragmentation through outside incitement. Only 51 percent of Iran's 65 million people are ethnic Persians, with ethnic Kurds, Azeris, Arabs, Baluch, and other groups forming a complex demographic mosaic throughout the country's provinces. Much has been made of Iran's ethnic fissures, yet the regime has proven surprisingly adept at co-opting ethnic minorities from the periphery into the center. As noted above, Former Defense Minister Ali Shamkhani is an ethnic Arab (on several occasions, he was dispatched by the Khatami administration to Khuzestan to allay Arab fears of marginalization), and the Supreme Leader 'Ali Khamenei himself is an Azeri.

Nonetheless, Iran has long feared agitation by its own Sunni and Arab populations. In light of growing tensions with the United States, fears of American and British support to ethnic Baluch separatists, Arab activists in Khuzestan, and Kurdish dissidents have grown more acute, and Iran has at times accused Saudi Arabia of supporting this effort among Arabs and Sunni Baluch.[68] Saudi analysts told RAND researchers in March 2007 that the presence of aggrieved minorities in Iran "could be useful leverage to the Kingdom. But so far we haven't exploited this."[69]

In the southwest province of Khuzestan, Iranian regime figures appear to perceive a sort of division of labor between Britain, which

---

[67] RAND interviews in Qatif, Damman, and al-Ahsa, March 2007.

[68] Among the significant ethnic groups, Azeris constitute 24 percent of the population, Kurds 7 percent, Arabs 3 percent, and Baluch 2 percent. For more on ethnic dissent in Iran, see John R. Bradley, "Iran's Ethnic Tinderbox," *Washington Quarterly*, Vol. 30, No. 1, Winter 2006–2007, pp. 181–190). RAND interview with a European scholar of Iran, October 2007.

[69] RAND interviews with Saudi former government officials and analysts, Jeddah, Saudi Arabia, March 2007.

they believe supplies lethal aid to ethnic Arab dissidents, and Saudi Arabia, which is thought to spread Salafi doctrine to subvert Iranians' religious outlook.[70] Tensions are also evident in eastern Iran, where the combination of weak administrative control by the government, drug smuggling, extremism, porous borders, and poverty have conspired to produce a low-grade insurgency by ethnic Baluch.[71] Not surprisingly, Saudi Arabia is frequently fingered as an external influence, given its widespread humanitarian and economic investment in the area, often in concert with Pakistan.[72]

In sum, manifestations of anti-Shi'a sentiments have risen since 2006, certainly among Saudi clerics and to a limited extent on the margins of the Saudi regime. Although this is certainly a religious issue for clerics, in a larger sense it reflects Saudi fears about the power vacuum that is opening up in Iraq. Thus it is more a political instrument than a religious difference, and its ultimate victims are Saudi Shi'as. For its part, Tehran has been hypersensitive about external meddling among its own ethnic and religious groups and probably attributes more omnipotence in this sphere to Saudi Arabia than is warranted.

---

[70] "Commentary Details Iran-Saudi Religious, Political Clash in Iraq," Persian Press, *Rahbord* (Tehran),), IAP20061113336001, 16 May 2006 [Commentary by Hamid Hadyan: "Exploring Iran-Saudi Arabia Relations in Light of New Regional Conditions"]; "Iranian Daily: Theologians Concerned by Reported Sunni Preaching in Khuzestan," *Aftab-e Yazd* (Tehran), translated by Open Source Center, IAP20051221011046, 20 December 2005; "Saudi Wahhabis Reportedly Funding Wahhabi Communities in Iran," Persian Press, [Report citing Jahan News Agency: "Wahhabis investing heavily in southern Iran"], Hezbollah (Tehran), translated by Open Source Center, IAP20071007011005, 2 October 2007.

[71] For more on the insurgency, see Alex Vatanka, "The Making of an Insurgency in Iran's Baluchestan Province," *Jane's Intelligence Review*, 1 June 2006.

[72] RAND interviews with analysts and officials in Dubai, UAE, February 2006, and with Saudi analysts, Riyadh, March 2007.

Managing Sectarianism: Saudi-Iranian Efforts to Regulate Tensions

Despite the increase in sectarian rhetoric described above, both states have made efforts to dampen sectarian tensions in their regional relationship.

Riyadh Has Taken Some Steps to Curtail Anti-Shi'a Pronouncements, but Will Continue a Policy of Ambivalence

In Saudi Arabia, King Abdullah appears to be an opponent of Salafi anti-Shi'a invective, but likely recognizes its occasional political utility. He must, moreover, contend with powerful domestic constituents who are more steadfast in their embrace of anti-Shiism. Our interviews in March 2007 suggest that it was Saudi Minister of Interior Prince Na'if who had tacitly given Salafi clerics an anti-Shi'a platform in exchange for their assistance in the regime's counterterrorism efforts against domestic jihadists.[73] As noted earlier, several Saudi interlocutors believed that sectarian identity was not itself an important fissure or marker within the general Saudi populace; the recurring problem was extremists on both sides, whose vociferous posturing tended to drown out voices of reconciliation and coexistence. According to one reformist,

> Sectarian dialogue in the Kingdom has progressed, thanks to maturity among the "center" on both sides. The Shi'as, for their part, have taken steps to marginalize "Shi'a racism" (*al-ta'assub al-Shi'i*) within their ranks. Nonetheless, extremists in both camps are the loudest and it often forces the moderates to retract.[74]

Among Saudi Shi'as, moderates such as Hassan al-Saffar, Ja'far al-Shayeb, and Mohammad Mahfouz have adopted dynamic new tactics

---

[73] RAND interviews with Saudi analysts and activists, Riyadh and Jeddah, March 2007. Scholar Yitzhak Nakash (2006) has also made this point, arguing that the al-Saud have frequently used anti-Shiism as a bridge to find common cause with Salafi clerics and deflect any criticism away from the regime itself.

[74] RAND interview with Saudi reformist, Riyadh, March 2007.

that focus on circumventing the regime-sanctioned channels, such as the National Dialogue, and building cross-sectarian ties. The ultimate goal, according to al-Saffar, is to create "space for the middle" and to diminish the appeal of sectarian mobilization as a popular strategy advanced by militant radicals in both camps. The apogee of this initiative occurred with al-Saffar's unprecedented visit to the Salafi strongholds of al-'Unayza and al-Qasim. Most recently, in June 2008, about 50 Saudi Shi'as performed Friday prayers at a Sunni mosque in al-Khobar; the historic event follows the participation of Sunni citizens in Friday prayers at a Shi'a mosque in al-Qatif. At the intellectual level, this push for reconciliation is illustrated by a 2007 edited volume published by Shi'a intellectual Mohammad Mahfouz entitled *al-Hiwar al-Madhhabi fi al-Mamlaka al-Arabiya al-Saudiya [Sectarian Dialogue in the Kingdom of Saudi Arabia]*. The book includes contributions from noted scholars from Sunni and Shi'a schools across the country—Malikis, Hanbalis, Shafi'is, Hanafis, Zaydis, Isma'ilis, and Twelver Shi'as.[75]

At the level of policy, Saudi Arabia has taken steps to prevent sectarianism from affecting its relations with Iran and, more broadly, from destabilizing key areas of the region. Much of this effort focuses on preventing Saudi volunteers from fighting in Iraq by suppressing clerical appeals that legitimate violent jihad as an obligation and encourage Sunni rancor against the Shi'as.[76] In October 2006, Riyadh hosted a meeting in Mecca, in which Sunni and Shi'a clerics issued a statement condemning sectarian violence in Iraq.[77] Gradually, Riyadh has evinced a markedly less sectarian slant to its policy in Iraq, with King Abdullah taking the groundbreaking step of meeting with Muqtada al-

---

[75] Mohammad Mahfouz, ed., *al-Hiwar al-Madhhabi fi al-Mamlaka al-Arabiya al-Saudiya [Sectarian Dialogue in the Kingdom of Saudi Arabia]*, Qatif, Saudi Arabia: Aafaq Center for Training and Studies, 2007.

[76] For example, "Saudi Mufti Lists Reasons for Warning Youths Against Seeking Jihad Abroad" (2007).

[77] "Iraqi Sunni and Shiite Clerics Sign Peace Appeal in Mecca," *Agence France-Press*, 20 October 2006. Also Donna Abu Nasr, "Saudi Arabia Treads Carefully as It Tries to Douse Threat of Sectarianism," Associated Press, 2 February 2007.

Sadr in January 2006.[78] In July 2007, Iraqi National Security Advisor Muwaffaq al-Ruba'i told the newspaper *al-Okaz* that he had reached an agreement with Saudi Interior Minister Na'if that both Iraq and Saudi Arabia would monitor sectarian *fatawa*.[79]

Nonetheless, the regime is likely to never completely eradicate anti-Shi'a sentiment and will probably continue a policy of ambivalence or tacit toleration.

Iran Has Been Critical of Saudi Arabia, but It Strives for Sectarian Unity

Iran's response to anti-Shi'a rhetoric from Saudi Arabia's clerics has been critical, differentiated and nuanced. As in the case of Saudi Arabia, there is an important split between official non-clerical voices, which have tended toward a more pragmatic focus on unity and preserving bilateral relations, and clerical figures both within and outside the regime, who have responded more forcefully. It is difficult to discern the views of Iran's most powerful figure, Supreme Leader Ali Khamenei, on Saudi Arabia, but he seems to be acting as arbiter and consensus-builder between pragmatic currents and those advocating a more confrontational stance toward the Kingdom—a role that has been a hallmark of his leadership style for nearly two decades. Although Khamenei has referred to the Saudi government as "evil," in the 1990s, he was willing to temper this outlook to support then-president Rafsanjani's efforts at rapprochement.[80]

While the Iranian government has publicly placed blame for these sectarian tensions elsewhere (namely the United States and "Zionism"), Iranian senior clerics, perhaps independently of the government, have responded strongly to perceived Saudi clerical incitements against the Shi'as. Their displeasure with Saudi Arabia reached a peak after the bombing of the al-Askari mosque in Samarra in 2006 and the re-bombing of the mosque's minarets in 2007.

---

[78] Norton (2007, pp. 436).

[79] "Iraq, Saudi to Monitor Sectarian Fatwas," *The Peninsula*, 16 July 2007.

[80] Karim Sadjadpour, *Reading Khamenei: The World View of Iran's Most Powerful Leader*, Washington, D.C.: Carnegie Endowment, March 2008, p. 14.

Responding to alleged Saudi *fatawa* calling for the destruction of Shi'a shrines, three of Qom's most senior clerics issued separate statements, published by the Iranian Students News Agency, directly attacking Saudi Arabia for its perceived role in encouraging the al-Askari bombing and for abetting "Wahhabi" violence against Iraqi Shi'as.[81] Grand Ayatollah Makarem Shirazi asked how Saudi Arabia could "permit its subjects to issue fatwas of death and terror that de-stabilize the world." He called for a dialogue with Saudi clerics to "familiarize" them with Islamic teachings, but also warned that if this did not to work, then the clerics should face "political and economic pressures." Makarem Shirazi also condemned the reported harassment of Shi'as in the "Prophet's mosque" in Medina.[82]

Grand Ayatollah Safi Golpaygani, a senior Qom cleric and widely recognized *marja'*, spoke against the "Wahhabi" sect for making "Islam and Muslims appear horrible to the rest of the world" and claimed that the "Wahhabis" had turned Mecca and Medina into "centers for the creation and export of terrorism."[83] He also questioned why countries such as Pakistan and Afghanistan should be under the "yoke" of the "Wahhabi" sect. Safi Golpaygani asked Iranian political officials to make "appropriate decisions" and "remind their friends, such as Syria, not to compromise with these terrorists."[84] Grand Ayatollah Nouri Hamedani also made similar statements condemning the Saudi government's complacency regarding the anti-Shi'a *fatawa*.

It is important to note that senior Iranian officials, perhaps eager to build friendlier relations with Saudi Arabia, have not blamed the Saudi government directly. Most notably, Supreme Leader Ayatollah Ali Khamenei in a June 2007 statement did not mention Saudi Arabia, Sunnis, or the Wahhabis, but rather blamed the "Zionists" and "occupiers" for the bombing of the Hadi al-Askari shrine in Samar-

---

[81] "Ayat Azam Makaram, Nouri va Safi dar mahkoumiyat e fatway e muftihaye Saudi [Grand Ayatollahs Makaram, Nouri, and Safi Condemn Fatwas Issued by Saudi Clerics]," Iranian Student News Agency, 23 July 2007).

[82] "Ayat Azam Makaram" (2007).

[83] "Ayat Azam Makaram" (2007).

[84] "Ayat Azam Makaram" (2007).

ra.[85] Khamenei, who has dubbed the Iranian calendar year ending in 2009 as one of *ensejam e Islami va vahdat meli* (Islamic solidarity and national unity), would like to maintain the image of unity between Sunnis and Shi'as.[86] Hence, he stressed that the al-Askari shrines "were respected in Samarra by Sunni Muslims for centuries and nobody had in any time insulted them."[87] The most visible expression of this push for cross-sectarian unity came in May 2008, with the convening in Tehran of the 21st Conference for Islamic Unity, chaired by Ayatollah Mohammad Ali Taskhiri, whom Khamenei had selected as the head of the World Forum for the Proximity of Islamic Schools of Thought.[88]

There has been acknowledgment of Saudi-Iran tensions, however, by unofficial but important political sources. The moderate Web site Entekhab News stated the Saudi King's official invitation for President Mahmoud Ahmadinejad to attend the Hajj trip to Mecca in 2008, was a sign that the "crisis and tensions between Sunnis and Shi'as have taken on a new dimension." According to Entekhab, the invitation offered "by the Sunni guardian of the holy shrines, the Saudi King, to the president of the only Shia country in the world . . . is a new effort to dispel the disagreements and religious tensions between the Sunnis

---

[85] Built in 944 C.E., the shrine's golden dome was destroyed in a bombing in February 2006, and the minarets were demolished in another attack in July 2007. The February bombing triggered a wave of sectarian violence in Iraq.

[86] Kamal Nazer Yasin, "Iran: Political and Religious Leaders Play the Nationalist Card," *Eurasia Insight*, 19 April 2007.

[87] "Zionists, Occupiers Behind Samarra Crime, Says Leader," Islamic Republic News Agency, 14 June 2007. Another important voice on cross-sectarian unity has been Iranian Parliament Speaker (and Khomeini's in-law), Gholam Ali Haddad-Adel. Haddad-Adel also blamed the Samarra bombings on "those who have gone on expedition to the Middle East, covetous of [regional] oil." He also expressed the hope that "Muslims in Iraq and other Islamic countries would enhance solidarity vigilantly to establish and guarantee unity and security in the oppressed country of Iraq." Haddad-Adel, who reportedly aspires to the presidency in Iran and may deal with the Saudis more extensively in the future, also avoided any mention of Saudi Arabia. See "Parliament Speaker Condemns Desecration of Shi'as' Shrines," Fars News Agency, 13 June 2007.

[88] For more on this outreach, see Alex Vatanka, "Iran's Shi'a Reach Out to Mainstream Salafists," *CTC Sentinel*, Vol. 1, No. 7, June 2008.

and Shias."[89] The article reveals that more moderate currents in Iran, who under President Khatami (1997–2005) had pursued a policy of rapprochement toward Saudi Arabia, may still have hope that tensions between Iran and Saudi Arabia can be reduced to a manageable level.

Inside Iran, it is also important to note that reducing these tensions has acquired a degree of political currency among some factions, particularly those opposed to Ahmadinejad. For example, a June 2008 opinion piece in a newspaper supportive of Ali Akbar Hashemi Rafsanjani's "Servants of Construction Party" claimed that the former president's visit to Saudi Arabia would improve the two countries' battered relations and result in a net victory for Iran. "Considering the al-Saud family's high regard for Hashemi-Rafsanjani," the editorial argues, "the visit can help reduce the tensions built up between the two neighbors over the past few years. That will be a huge help to the ninth government's foreign policy."[90]

The Hajj Is a Venue for Sectarian Rivalry, but Also Commonality

The dynamics of sectarian tension and cooperation outlined above are illustrated in the handling of the Hajj (pilgrimage to Mecca), which has been a long-standing source of ideological tension, but has also emerged as a venue for dialogue and symbolic rapprochement.

Bilateral differences certainly exist over the Hajj. These are mostly over access, quotas for Iranian pilgrims, their mistreatment, and their agitation against the Saudis—issues that were symbolically significant enough to contribute to the termination of diplomatic relations from 1988 to 1991. In the mid-1990s, contention over the Hajj continued to buffet the progress toward substantive rapprochement, with Tehran frequently accusing Riyadh of cutting quotas for Iranians or denying Iranian pilgrims the right to hold anti-American political rallies; the latter issue proved especially expeditious for Iran's leaders to lambaste

---

[89] Entekhab News, "Tasbiyat ghodrat e Iran ba didar Ahmadinejad is Mecca, [Ahamdinejad's Visit to Mecca Strengthens Iran's Power]" 28 December 2007b.

[90] Open Source Center, Persian Press: Commentary Argues Saudis Seek Improved Ties with Rafsanjani Visit; IAP20080616011005 Tehran *Hamshahri* in Persian 11 Jun 08 p 17 (Unattributed commentary from the "Politics" column: "Outcome of Rafsanjani's Saudi Visit").

the al-Saud as U.S. puppets.[91] Today, there are resurgent accusations in the Iranian press and by officials of mistreatment of Iranian pilgrims by hard-line Salafis or by the regime itself.[92] Most recently, in June 2008, Iranian press outlets accused Saudi Arabia of harassing married Iranian pilgrims and Iranian clerics. The fingerprinting of Iranian pilgrims—a practice reportedly instituted in late 2007—has drawn particular ire from Iran.[93]

Yet the pilgrimage is also a venue for smoothing over differences, at least symbolically. Iranian president Ahmadinejad's performance of the Hajj in December 2007 at the invitation of King Abdullah best illustrates this. Still, each side used the occasion to implicitly trumpet their regional primacy. An Iranian cleric heralded the visit as "proof" of Iran's regional popularity, and during the visit Iranian pilgrims were seen on videotape holding placards proclaiming, "Death to America and Israel"—no doubt more than a slight embarrassment to the al-Saud. Saudi Arabia for its part portrayed itself as the magnanimous host. A year later, coinciding with Rafsanjani's visit in June 2008, Saudi authorities allowed Iranian female pilgrims to visit a revered Shi'a cemetery in Medina for the first time.[94]

These efforts at accommodation show how sectarian concord provides each country as much of a platform for political maneuvering as sectarian tension does.

---

[91] "Iranian-Saudi Row Reignites Again, Focusing on Pilgrimage Dispute," *Mideast Mirror*, Vol. 8, No. 52, 16 March 1994.

[92] "Iranian Pilgrims Reportedly Mistreated by Hardline Salafis," Tehran Raja News, translated by Open Source Center, IAP2008010101606001, 31 December 2007.

[93] BBC Monitoring, "Iran Paper Says Saudi Agents Wage 'Psychological Warfare' Against Iranian Pilgrims," Mardom-Salari Web site, 11 July 2007; BBC Monitoring, "Saudi Arabia Fingerprints Iranian Student Pilgrims," Fars News Agency, 11 July 2008.

[94] BBC Monitoring Middle East, "Iran Women Pilgrims Visit Baqi Cemetery in Medina for First Time—Agency," 9 June 2008. The cemetery, known as Jannat al-Baqi (The Gate of Heaven) contains the graves of many of the Prophet Mohammad's companions. It was demolished in 1925 by Ibn Saud.

Conclusion: Sectarianism and Ideology Shape Relations, but Do Not Define Them

Shi'a-Sunni tensions and ideological differences are important factors in the Saudi-Iranian relationship, which shape the two states' policy outlooks and behavior throughout the Middle East. Yet as this chapter has demonstrated, they are not the principle determinant that predisposes the two countries toward confrontation. For both countries, ideology and religion have a certain instrumentality and utility—regimes in Tehran and Riyadh can emphasize, highlight, or minimize differences to serve broader geopolitical aims.

Since 2003 and especially since the ascendancy of President Ahmadinejad in Iran, Iran's policy outlook has been marked by a sense of triumphalism and an activist embrace of pan-Arab causes, most notably the Israeli-Palestinian issue. Combined with its defiance of the West on the nuclear issue, Iran has acquired an appeal that has on occasion transcended sectarian differences. This appeal represents an indirect critique of the al-Saud, who are perceived by regional and domestic opponents as being too cautious and deferential to the West. For their part, rulers in Riyadh have been confronted with anti-Shi'a pressures from their own Salafi clerical establishment, but they have also knowingly harnessed this rhetoric to deflect Iran's more populist and anti–status quo appeal. The consequences of this sectarian strategy have been most visibly felt inside Saudi Arabia, among the Kingdom's own Shi'a population. At the same time, both states have shown an interest in dampening sectarian tensions, if only in the service of larger political and geostrategic aims.

The next chapters show how the dynamics of Saudi-Iranian relations play out in the larger political and geostrategic contexts of the Gulf region and the Levant (Lebanon and Palestine).

CHAPTER THREE

Relations in the "Core": Conflict Regulation in the Gulf and Iraq

In light of the previous framework for assessing sectarian and ideological fissures, this chapter will explore Saudi-Iranian relations in the "Core"—the immediate geographical neighborhood of the two countries, which includes the Persian Gulf and Iraq.

First, we examine how Saudi Arabia and Iran play out their aspirations in the Gulf and how Gulf states recognize and react to Riyadh and Tehran's interests and perceptions. A critical theme is that disunity among the GCC states, exemplified most starkly by Qatar and Oman's historically independent foreign policy postures, has had the effect of moderating Saudi-Iranian relations. In effect, Saudi Arabia and Iran are each competing to manage and woo the GCC—overtures that have important implications for U.S. efforts to construct a bloc-like front against Iran. Second, we canvass three other sources of bilateral tension between Iran and Saudi Arabia—Iraq, Iran's nuclear program, and oil and gas issues—that have affected Gulf stability and drawn differing policy reactions from the GCC.

Taken in sum, Saudi-Iranian relations in the Gulf since 2003 suggest the propensity of the two states to manage their threat perceptions and to allow more pragmatic concerns to temper their rivalry. Certainly, as the last chapter has shown, sectarian tension arising from the situation in Iraq and events in Lebanon has affected Shi'a-Sunni communities in Kuwait, Bahrain, and Saudi Arabia and ultimately strained the relationship between Saudi Arabia and Iran. But a range of other bilateral interests, along with the persistent ability of smaller

GCC states to thwart Saudi attempts at building a bloc-like containment structure, have resulted in relations that are characterized more by a mixture of accommodation and wary engagement than by pure confrontation.

Disunity and Diversity in the GCC Have Tempered Bilateral Relations

The Saudis have become less focused on the GCC's development as a coherent organization, realizing that member governments' determination to maintain control over their own monetary policy, defense, and trade places a firm constraint on progress toward integration.[1] There is also significant disarray in policy toward Iran, with states weighing the risks of confrontation and a military strike against the current economic opportunities afforded by the status quo, however undesirable.[2]

More importantly, GCC threat perceptions are informed by a tendency to overestimate Iran's military threat and to underestimate their own capabilities. As noted in the previous chapter, Iran's principal threat

---

[1]   For historical context behind the smaller Gulf states' suspicion of Saudi Arabia, see Rosemarie Said Zahlan, *The Making of the Modern Gulf States: Kuwait, Bahrain, Qatar, the United Arab Emirates and Oman*, London, England: Ithaca Press, 1998, pp. 135–155. For a discussion of the shortcomings of the GCC, see Michael N. Barnett and F. Gregory Gause, III, "Caravans in Opposite Directions: Society, State, and the Development of Community in the Gulf Cooperation Council," in Emanuel Adler and Michael N. Barnett, eds., *Security Communities*, Cambridge Studies in International Relations, Cambridge, England: Cambridge University Press, 1998.

[2]   For analysis, see "UK Daily Views Gulf Arabs' Dilemma Over Response to Iran's Suspected Ambitions, London, *The Financial Times*, EUP20070102167006, 1 January 2007; "Analysis of GCC Countries' Stances Toward Possible US-Iran War," *al-Sharq al-Awsat* (London), translated by Open Source Center, GMP20070923913004, 23 September 2007 [Article by Abd-al-Rahman al-Rashid (Part 1 of 2): "Will the Gulf Countries Remain Neutral in the War?"]; Salman al-Durusi, "Al-Shaykh Khalifah bin Salman: Al-Khalij La Yatahammal Harb Jadidah [Shaykh Khalifah Bin Salman: The Gulf Cannot Take Another War]," *Al-Sharq Al-Awsat*, 28 July 2007; and Hasan Fahs, "Abd al-Hadi LilHayat: Ay Sidam Irani-Amriki Sayas'ub Dhabtuhu Li'an Sahatuhu Wasi'ah wa al-Imkanat Kabira [Abd al-Hadi to al-Hayat Newspaper: Any American-Iranian Confrontation Would Be Difficult to Contain Because the Front Is Wide and the Resources Are Huge]," *al-Hayat*, 9 February 2007.

to Gulf regimes is an ideological and asymmetric one: its efforts to seize the moral high ground on the Palestine issue, its support for regional militancy by Hamas and Hizballah, and its alleged ability to mobilize disenfranchised Shi'as. While not a physical danger to Gulf leaders, these tactics present an indirect critique of their legitimacy to regional and domestic audiences—which can be just as worrisome as a conventional military attack.[3] In addition, some of the GCC's heightened threat perception may be calculated to forestall any U.S.-Iranian rapprochement, which Gulf regimes may, in the long term, fear more than a U.S.-Iranian war. As summarized by one Arab columnist, "The Arab countries in the Gulf fear Iranian ambitions, worry about an Iranian-American military confrontation, and fear an agreement between the two countries," which would result in Gulf states being sidelined.[4]

For its part, Tehran has long viewed Saudi Arabia as an obstacle to Iran taking its place as the preeminent power in the Gulf. For example, an editorial on the Web site Baztab, affiliated with former Revolutionary Guards Commander Mohsen Rezai, noted: "The Saudis are seeking to exclude Iran's domination in the Middle East."[5] To circumvent this obstacle, Iran has repeatedly called for an indigenous system that would exclude U.S. involvement and implicitly relegate Saudi Arabia to the status of a junior partner.[6] When Iran does make reference to multilateralism in the Gulf, it is usually careful to refer to a "Persian Gulf Security System," even though Tehran likely realizes this idea is a non-starter for the Gulf Arab states.[7]

---

[3] F. Gregory Gause III, "Threats and Threat Perceptions in the Persian Gulf Region," *Middle East Policy*, Vol. 14, No. 2, Summer 2007b.

[4] Jihad al-Khazin, "Al-Maradh al-Arabi [The Arab Disease]," Saudi in Focus Web site, 6 April 2007.

[5] Quoted in Kaveh Afrasiabi, "Saudi-Iran Tension Fuels Wider Conflict," *Asia Times*, 6 December 2006.

[6] Shahram Chubin, *Iran's Nuclear Ambitions*, Washington, D.C.: Carnegie, 2006, p. 118; also, "Ruyarui-e Iran va Arabestan dar khavar-e miane [Iran and Saudi Arabia Confrontation in the Middle East]" (2006).

[7] For an example, "Iranian Official Says Tehran Ready to Hold 'Multilateral' Talks with GCC Nations," *Islamic Republic News Agency* (Tehran), translated by Open Source Center, IAP20051203011031, 3 December 2005.

In tandem with this approach, Iran has sought to bolster its bilateral relations with the smaller GCC states in order to exploit tensions between those states and Saudi Arabia and to erode Saudi influence.[8] Tehran appears to evince a special appreciation for how disunity in the GCC and antagonism toward Saudi Arabia present an opportunity to thwart Riyadh's designs. One study from *Aftab News* argues that the GCC has failed to achieve its objectives of integration precisely because Saudi Arabia has disproportionate power, rooted in its larger territory, population, gross national product, and military might and underscored by the fact that the permanent location of the GCC secretariat is in Saudi Arabia.[9] Such a view is precisely the crack that Tehran seeks to widen in its relations with individual Gulf states.

Gulf actors themselves have responded in different ways to these approaches, and it is important to consider their respective policies as we seek to understand the larger implications of Saudi-Iranian relations for that region. The following country-by-country analysis highlights each state's perception of its role in the contending regional orders articulated by Saudi Arabia and Iran.

Qatar Has Exploited Tensions with Iran to Balance Saudi Arabia

Perhaps more than any other Gulf state, Qatar has exploited Saudi-Iranian competition to carve out a highly independent, proactive, and, at times, seemingly paradoxical foreign policy.[10] Many of its policies toward Iran or toward regional conflicts involving Iran appear designed to balance, or even subvert, the influence of its historical rival, Saudi

---

[8] For background, see Mark Gasiorowski, "The New Aggressiveness in Iran's Foreign Policy," *Middle East Policy*, Vol 14, No. 2, Summer 2007.

[9] "Negahi be sheklgiriye shoraye hamkariye khalije fars: Etehadi ke az jange Iran va aragh motevalled shod [A Look at the Establishment of the Persian Gulf Cooperation Council: A Cooperation Born as a Result of Iran-Iraq War]," *Aftab News*, 7 July 2006.

[10] As the seat of U.S. Central Command, Doha hosts the largest U.S. military presence in the region, yet also controls the pan-Arab satellite TV station *al-Jazeera*, which has frequently given air time to al-Qaeda and taken a sympathetic line toward anti-U.S. insurgents in Iraq.

Arabia.[11] It was Doha's invitation to Ahmadinejad to the 2007 GCC Summit in Doha that effectively shifted the Gulf approach toward Iran from one of bloc-like containment to accommodation. Although Saudi Foreign Minister Saud al-Faysal appeared to tacitly endorse this move, there was strong criticism from the editor of the Saudi-owned *al-Sharq al-Aswat*, who in previous editorials had lambasted Qatar as a "microphone state."[12]

Much of Riyadh's rancor toward the tiny state has been directly principally toward its control of *al-Jazeera*, which has sounded a steady drumbeat of anti-Saudi themes and frequently hosted Saudi oppositionists. Severe problems were apparent even before Riyadh's September 2002 announcement that it was recalling its ambassador to Doha, Hamad al-Tuwaymi, following a row over *al-Jazeera*. A few months earlier Saudi media had advised Doha to "reconsider its policies" regarding *al-Jazeera*—Riyadh had been particularly offended by a televised debate in June 2002 in which participants had criticized then Crown Prince Abdullah's peace initiative. Riyadh timed its ambassadorial recall to coincide with Qatar's National Day.

In late 2007, however, the two states took steps to mend their differences, fueled principally by a shared concern about Iranian reprisals for a U.S. attack. In mid-2007, close advisors to the Supreme Leader made a number of highly public statements about retaliating against the Gulf states in the event of a U.S. strike on Iran's nuclear facilities.[13] In September, Emir Shaykh Hamad Bin Khalifa al-Thani, accompanied by Qatari Prime Minister and Foreign Minister Shaykh Hamad Bin Jassim Bin Jabr al-Thani, traveled to Jeddah for talks with King

---

[11] The history of tensions between the two states stems back to the early state-building efforts of Ibn Saud and his claim on Qatari territory, which prompted Qatar's ruler, Shaykh Abdallah bin Qasim, to sign a treaty with Britain as a form of protection. The border between the two states was never officially demarcated. In the mid-1990s, there were continuing disputes between the two states about GCC leadership.

[12] *Al-Sharq al-Awsat*, 27 March 2007.

[13] Michael Smith, "Iran Threatens Gulf Blitz If U.S. Hits Nuclear Plant" *The Times* (London), 10 June 2007.

Abdullah.[14] In subsequent months, *al-Jazeera* toned down its previously hostile programming toward Saudi Arabia.

In addition to engaging with Saudi Arabia, Qatar has been making careful diplomatic overtures to Iran and has worked with Tehran on a number of fronts outside of the Gulf, particularly on Lebanon and Syria. These initiatives illustrate Doha's historic approach to accommodating Iran, making vocal acknowledgements of its status as a "neighbor" and not an "enemy," while at the same time prudently bolstering its defenses as a form of insurance.[15] As will be discussed in the next chapter, Qatar successfully mediated a resolution to Lebanon's political deadlock that involved factions backed by both Tehran and Riyadh. In addition, Qatar was the only country to reject a U.N. Security Council resolution calling for Tehran to halt uranium enrichment.[16]

But Doha's accommodation of Iran has not completely mitigated the underlying sources of tension. For example, a major diplomatic row occurred in 2006 between the two countries when Qatar's emir called the Gulf "Arabian" and not "Persian." Beyond this rhetorical tension, another source of disagreement is the sharing of the offshore gas reserve of the North Field (the largest natural gas reserve in the world, with 25 trillion cubic meters). This issue is likely to grow in importance between the two countries, particularly as the Iranian economy worsens.[17]

As of January 2009, it appeared that Qatari-Saudi tensions had surfaced once again over Israel's December 2008 incursion into Gaza. Doha and Riyadh held near-simultaneous meetings of Arab leaders, with Qatar taking the additional step of inviting Ahmadinejad, Syria's Bashar al-Assad, Iraq's vice president Tariq al-Hashemi, and Hamas

---

[14] Significantly, the chairman of *al-Jazeera*'s board, Shaykh Hamad bin Thamer al-Thani, was also among the delegates to Jeddah. Robert F. Worth, "Al-Jazeera No Longer Nips at the Saudis," *The New York Times*, 4 January 2008.

[15] Domestic constituents probably factor into the regime's approach toward Iran; an estimated 30 to 40 percent of Qatari citizens are of Iranian descent.

[16] See United Nations Security Council, "Security Council Demands Iran Suspend Uranium Enrichment by 31 August, or Face Possible Economic, Diplomatic Sanctions," 21 July 2006.

[17] Olivier Guitta, "First Target for Iran: Qatar?" *Middle East Times*, 26 November 2007.

leader Khaled Mishal to the Arab League summit in Doha. Egypt and Saudi Arabia refused to attend. At a subsequent emergency meeting of the GCC in Kuwait, Qatar joined Syria in opposing the revival of King Abdullah's 2002 peace initiative. In the Saudi-sponsored press, the response was predictable; familiar themes about "upstart" Qatar and its malign effect on Arab unity reappeared, with one commentator calling the Doha meeting a "summit of divisions."[18] Iran, for its part, was quick to highlight this acrimony, painting Saudi Arabia as the odd man out at the Arab League summit.[19]

Qatar's continued ability to rally a competing Arab consensus against the one sought by Riyadh shows how structural tensions inside the GCC can temper the Saudi-Iranian relationship.

Oman's Accommodating Stance Toward Iran Diverges Sharply from Saudi Arabia's

Like Qatar, Oman has sought to play off Saud-Iranian relations to carve out a sovereign niche in Gulf affairs; the strategically-located sultanate has historically navigated a delicate course between engagement with Iran, suspicion of Saudi Arabia, and a preference for strong bilateral ties with the United States.

Similar to Qatar, Oman has long enjoyed close relations with Iran, stemming from its proximity and shared sense of culture, history, and trade. Between 1970 and 1977, Omani ruler Sultan Qaboos acknowledged Iran's regional strength and obtained Iranian military assistance in fighting an insurgency in Oman's underdeveloped province of Dhofar. In a meeting with RAND researchers, a senior Omani military officer argued that this support continues to inform Oman's perceptions of Iran; it occurred during a critical period "when the rest of our Arab allies abandoned us."[20] During the same period, an Omani-Iranian border agreement was also signed regarding the Strait of Hormuz. Today, an Omani-Iranian Joint Military Committee meets

---

[18] For example, Radwan al-Said, "Qimat al-Inqisam al-Arabi ... Hal Tan'aqid? [The Summit of Divisions ... Will It Convene?] al-Sharq al-Awsat, 16 January 2009.

[19] See "Saudi Arabia Dislikes High-Level Gaza Summit," Press TV, 14 January 2009.

[20] RAND interview with a retired military official, Muscat, Oman, February 2006.

regularly to discuss security issues, including the security of the Strait. Citing this forum and also Sultan Qaboos's reported role in facilitating the early 1990s rapprochement between Riyadh and Tehran, a retired Omani military officer opined that Oman could serve as a potential diplomatic "bridge" between Iran and Saudi Arabia.[21]

Speaking on the Iranian nuclear issue, a number of current and retired Omani officials downplayed the threat from Tehran and pointed instead to what one interlocutor called Saudi Arabia's "hegemonic overreaction to Iran" as the greater danger.[22] Fueling this suspicion is Oman's resentment of Saudi Arabia over its claim to the disputed Buraymi Oasis and its support to anti-regime insurgents in western Oman during the 1960s. "The Kingdom of Saudi Arabia is an expansive state that is constantly moving frontiers to grab oil," noted one Omani official.[23] One result of this hostility has been Oman's frequent reluctance to embrace collective security measures against Iran, which it sees as a thinly disguised front for Saudi dominance of Gulf affairs.[24] As noted by another interlocutor, "Oman's preference for bilateralism is rooted in history: the Damascus Declaration and the GCC's Peninsula Shield Force were dissolved. In the last 20 years there is a history of poor coordination among local states."[25]

---

[21] RAND interview, Muscat, Oman, February 2006.

[22] RAND interview with retired Omani diplomat, Muscat, Oman, February 2006.

[23] RAND interview, Muscat, Oman, February 2006.

[24] For background on Oman's posture toward Saudi Arabia, see Joseph A. Kechichian, *Oman and the World: The Emergence of an Independent Foreign Policy*, Santa Monica, Calif.: RAND Corporation, 1995, pp. 66–76.

[25] RAND interview, Muscat, Oman, February 2006. The Peninsula Shield was a largely symbolic attempt at a joint GCC defense force, established in 1986 and dissolved in 2005. There was frequent disagreement among the GCC about command and control and other parameters of operation, with Kuwait, Oman, and the UAE frequently voicing concern about Saudi Arabia's dominance. The Damascus Declaration was a similarly ephemeral attempt at GCC defense through partnership with Egypt and Syria after the 1991 Gulf war. See Matteo Legrenzi, "The Peninsula Shield Force: End of a Symbol?" *Gulf Research Center Insights*, Issue 3, July 2006, and Rosemary Hollis, "Whatever Happened to the Damascus Declaration," in M. Jane Davis, ed., *Politics and International Relations in the Middle East*, Aldershot, England: Edward Elgar, 1995.

Taken in sum, these factors make Oman's outlook unique on the Arabian Peninsula and frequently compel it to act in sharp divergence from Saudi initiatives toward Iran.

Bahrain Is a Source of Contention Because of Iran's Historical Claim and Sectarian Tensions

Bahrain is a source of contention between Saudi Arabia and Iran, both for historical and sectarian reasons. Shi'a-Sunni tensions are a particular concern in Bahrain, which is arguably the Peninsula's epicenter of sectarian disenfranchisement. Shi'as make up 70 percent of the population, are ruled over by the Sunni al-Khalifa family, and have long suffered from political exclusion, unemployment, housing shortages, and, to a lesser extent, cultural discrimination. The presence of the U.S. Fifth Fleet in Manama is a further complication in the Saudi-Iranian bilateral relationship. As noted earlier, Tehran has traditionally held the al-Saud responsible for hosting U.S. forces in the Gulf and likely sees Bahrain's al-Khalifa as acting under Saudi influence, if not direction.

Traditionally, these dynamics have made Bahrain an attractive arena for Iranian retaliation or subversion that has been at least partly aimed at Saudi Arabia. In the early 1980s, for example, Bahraini authorities announced the discovery of a coup plot by Shi'a dissidents who had been allegedly trained and funded by Iran. Iran's aggressive policies toward Bahrain diminished in the 1990s, the result of Rafsanjani's shift toward pragmatism and Khatami's subsequent efforts at rapprochement with Saudi Arabia and the broader Gulf. With the recent spike in U.S.-Iranian tensions over the nuclear issue, the Bahraini regime has once again begun to suspect the presence of Bahraini Shi'a sleeper cells beholden to Iran.[26] However, some analysts have pointed out that, with the relative proximity of U.S. forces and assets in neighboring Iraq, Bahrain's traditional attractiveness as an arena of Iranian retaliation or subversion has declined.

---

[26] Author's discussion with a Bahraini official, 13 November 2006, Manama, Bahrain. This official noted that "there is no doubt that Iran and Hizballah are instigating something we've never seen. But we can absorb it through economic reforms."

Relations between Manama and Tehran suffered a setback in July 2007 after Hussain Shariatmadari, editor of the Iranian newspaper *Kayhan*, argued that Bahrain was an inseparable part of Iran.[27] The tension eased after Tehran insisted that these remarks did not represent its official policy, and the foreign ministers of both countries said that bilateral relations remained strong and would not be harmed by these comments. Nevertheless, more than 500 Bahrainis, including Sunni clerics and lawmakers, gathered outside the Iranian Embassy in Bahrain to protest the statement.[28] Calm eventually prevailed, and as of late 2008, Iranian-Bahraini relations had warmed to the point where the two states had renewed a five-year security agreement covering terrorism and narcotics.[29] But the *Kayhan* incident demonstrates how Iran's historical claims to the archipelago and the echo effect of its nationalist rhetoric can affect Bahrain's domestic stability and amplify tensions with Riyadh.

Saudi Arabia has also evinced a somewhat proprietary view toward Bahrain, rooted in the al-Khalifa's tribal roots in Saudi Arabia and also the oil subsidies that Riyadh provides to Bahrain. Yet, as in Oman and Qatar, officials in Saudi Arabia have been frequently exasperated by Bahrain's go-it-alone approach, epitomized most starkly by Bahrain's signing of a free trade agreement with the United States. There is also Saudi concern about how the al-Khalifa family has responded to Bahraini Shi'a dissent. At the height of the mid-1990s uprising in Bahrain—inspired partly by Shi'a economic discontent—Riyadh threatened to intervene militarily if the violence was not suppressed. There were reports of similar warnings during Shi'a unrest in 2007. At the other end of the spectrum, Riyadh is concerned that Manama's efforts to accommodate the Shi'as through political reform is a dangerous game that offers increased openings for Iranian influence. A Saudi offi-

---

[27] *Kayhan* is widely regarded as a semi-official mouthpiece of Supreme Leader Khamenei. See also "Jesarate padeshahe Bahrain be jazayere Irani! [Bahrain's King Impudence about the Iranian Islands!]," *Aftab News*, 18 December 2006, which attacks Bahrain's king for statements about the "Arabian" Gulf.

[28] "Bahrainis Protest Against Iran Province Claim," *Reuters*, 14 July 2007.

[29] "Iran," Press TV, 25 December 2008.

cial in the Gulf told RAND researchers, "We are watching the [2006] Bahraini parliamentary elections very closely. The hand of Iran is very strong."[30] For their part, some factions of the al-Khalifa have pointed to Saudi pressure as a reason why the Bahraini regime cannot proceed quickly on liberalization—although several Bahraini activists have disputed this, calling it a convenient excuse for deferring on reform.[31]

These dynamics reveal that political stability in Bahrain is closely linked to the state of tensions between Riyadh and Tehran. One important result is that Manama will increasingly pursue a sort of triangular diplomacy that involves bolstering bilateral ties with the United States to counterbalance pressures from both Iran *and* Saudi Arabia.[32]

Kuwait Has Tended Closer to Saudi Arabia's Position on Iran Than Other Gulf States

Kuwait's position toward Iran has been closer to that of Saudi Arabia's than those of Oman, the UAE, and Qatar.[33] The shared threat from Iraq during the 1990s cemented Kuwaiti-Saudi ties, and both countries have been concerned about Iranian drilling of the Kuwait/Saudi offshore oilfield at Dorra.[34] Although Kuwait is working patiently with

---

[30] RAND interview with a Saudi official in the Gulf, November 2006. This same official, however, opined that Riyadh could ultimately live with a Shi'a prime minister in Bahrain, arguing that Manama's continued dependence on Saudi oil subsidies and the nationalist bent of most Bahraini Shi'as would prevent the country from falling into Tehran's orbit.

[31] RAND interviews in Manama, Bahrain, November 2006. Also 'Abd al-Nabi al-Ukri, "Mutatallabat wa Tab'iat al-Islah al-Khaliji [Requirements and Development of Reform in the Gulf]," unpublished, undated paper provided to the authors, Manama, Bahrain, November 2006.

[32] For background on this diplomatic approach, see Fred H. Lawson, *Bahrain: The Modernization of Autocracy*, Boulder, Colorado: Westview Press, 1989, pp. 117–134.

[33] Commenting on the GCC's disarray toward Iran, a Kuwaiti scholar lamented that "the Omanis are on another planet." RAND interview with a Kuwaiti scholar, Kuwait City, February 2006.

[34] Kuwaiti-Iranian ties strengthened slightly after the 1991 Gulf war, but in the wake of the 2003 ouster of Saddam, bilateral relations have grown tenser. For background, see Abdullah K. al-Shayji, "Mutual Realities, Perceptions and Impediments Between the GCC States and Iran," in Lawrence Potter and Gary G. Sick, eds., *Security in the Persian Gulf: Origins, Obstacles and the Search for Consensus*, New York: PalgraveMacmillan, 2002.

Saudi Arabia and Iran over energy issues and is actively negotiating the future of several petroleum and natural gas contracts with each country, it has been caught in a cycle of threats and counter-threats from both Riyadh and Tehran.[35] Iran has warned Kuwait that it will be targeted with missile attacks if the United States attacks Iran. In the wake of these threats, Saudi officials, specifically Crown Prince Sultan, have rushed to Kuwait City to reassure the Kuwaitis that Saudi Arabia will protect them in any such conflict.

As with all Gulf states, Kuwait has had to decide on an appropriate posture on the Iranian nuclear issue. A chief concern in Kuwait is its proximity to Iran's Bushehr reactor and the threat to the Kuwaiti economy from even a minuscule leakage of radioactive material.[36] According to a seasoned Kuwaiti diplomat, Kuwait's current approach rests on four principles:

- showing diplomatic support for the EU-3 and U.S. (the P5+1) efforts to talk Iran out of its nuclear ambitions through the use of sanctions
- working to build consensus within the GCC on trying to convey to Tehran the disadvantages of nuclear acquisition
- supporting further opposition to the nuclear program via the United Nations Security Council
- engaging Iran on a bilateral basis and encouraging non–Middle Eastern states, such as India and China, to do the same.[37]

Sectarian tensions have generally not been a factor in Kuwaiti-Iranian relations. The political inclusion of Kuwaiti Shi'as (one-quarter of Kuwait's population of one million) in the country's nascent democratic processes has drawn applause from reformists in neighboring

---

[35] RAND interviews, UAE, December 2007, February 2008.

[36] RAND interview with a Kuwaiti think-tank scholar, Kuwait City, February 2006. See also the lecture by the Kuwait foreign minister Shaykh Mohammad Sabah Al-Salem Al-Sabahat reported "Kuwait News Agency–Concerns over Bushehr: Kuwait Raises Israeli Nukes," International Institute for Strategic Studies, 20 November 2006

[37] RAND interview with a senior Kuwaiti diplomat, Kuwait City, February 2006.

states.[38] Although Kuwait during the 1980s suffered from Iranian-inspired agitation by Shi'a dissidents, it is frequently cited as the Gulf's "success story" of Shi'a integration.[39] One Kuwaiti activist noted to RAND researchers in 2006,

> Kuwait's Shi'a population is not susceptible to Iranian appeals. The Kuwaiti government is working to bolster national loyalty among its Shi'a citizens. The government's trust in the Shi'a increased dramatically following the 1991 Iraqi invasion, when the Shi'a played a heroic role in the resistance.[40]

Yet this harmony was disrupted in the wake of the assassination of Hizballah military commander Imad Mughniyah in Damascus in February 2008.[41] The presence of two Kuwaiti Shi'a parliamentarians at a commemorative rally for Mughniyah prompted Sunni lawmakers to suspect the existence of a secret Hizballah cell in Kuwait, supposedly working to destroy the foundations of society and thus, implicitly, to overthrow the government.[42] The Mughniyah episode shows that Iran's involvement in the Arab-Israeli issue has affected not only Saudi Arabia's regional legitimacy but the domestic tranquility of other Gulf countries. In light of this dynamic, it is not surprising that Kuwaiti officials frequently press for a resolution of the Palestinian-Israeli dispute to mitigate the threat from Iran. "Solve the Palestinian issue," one Kuwaiti diplomat argued, "and you'll de-fang Iran in the region."[43]

---

[38] Bahraini Shi'a activists frequently pointed to the Kuwaiti constitution as a model for emulation. Jill Crystal, "Political Reform and the Prospects for Democratic Transition in the Gulf," *Fundación para leas Relaciones Internacionales ye el Diálogo Exterior (FRIDE)*, Working Paper, 11 July 2005.

[39] Louër (2008), pp. 45–65. It is important to note that most of the terrorism conducted on Kuwaiti soil was by Iraqi Shi'as, rather than Kuwaitis.

[40] RAND interview with a Kuwaiti lawyer and reform activist, Kuwait City, February 2006.

[41] Mughniyah was known to be a prime suspect for terror activity against Kuwait in the 1980s.

[42] The arrested lawmakers were subsequently released in late 2008 for lack of evidence.

[43] RAND interview with a Kuwaiti diplomat, Kuwait City, February 2006.

Despite the Islands Dispute, the United Arab Emirates Has Increasingly Acted as an Intermediary

The posture of the UAE toward both Iran and Saudi Arabia is more nuanced and multidimensional than is commonly accepted. Much of this stems from the often overlooked differences in priorities and outlooks of the member emirates.

The UAE's territorial dispute with Iran over Abu Musa and the Greater and Lesser Tunbs islands is frequently cited as the major source of tension with Tehran, and the member emirates have been generally united on this issue at the formal diplomatic level. Yet privately and informally, Emiratis display varying degrees of attachment to the islands, with several interlocutors noting that the dispute is predominately a concern for Abu Dhabi.[44] Dubai's relations with Iran have traditionally been warmer given its proximity to an Iranian attack, the influence of Iranian investment, and its Iranian expatriate population, numbering nearly half a million. In addition, some of Dubai's most prominent and influential merchant families (e.g., the Galadari) are of Iranian ancestry. During the Iran-Iraq war, for example, Dubai's position toward Tehran was noticeably softer than that of the other emirates. Dubai has also traditionally opposed any strengthening of the GCC's joint military force because this would empower Abu Dhabi.[45] One Emirati interlocutor opined to RAND that this divergence presents a dangerous diplomatic "wedge" for Iran to exploit, particularly in the event of a conflict with the United States.[46]

Other emirates fall somewhere in the middle of this spectrum: Sharjah is influenced by Saudi Arabia, while Ras al-Khaimah and Umm al-Quwain have cultivated increasingly closer ties to Iran. An Emirati civil service official noted that, given this internal diversity, the UAE's posture as a whole toward Iran has alternated between the twin

---

[44] One interlocutor asserted that Abu Dhabi was able to take a more hard-line view on Iran because it is the emirate with the most strategic depth from an Iranian strike. RAND interview with an Emirati academic, Sharjah, February 2006.

[45] Each emirate has long maintained its own national guard. The debate over command and control and integration has been the strongest between Abu Dhabi and Dubai.

[46] RAND interview with a UAE scholar, Sharjah, February 2006.

poles of "accommodation and hostility." "There is the islands dispute," this official stated, "but the UAE is also Iran's biggest trading partner. We take a balanced approach toward Iran."[47]

This middle ground position has resulted in the UAE emerging as a sort of neutral forum for Iran, Saudi Arabia, and the United States to make pronouncements on the regional order—a role perhaps best exemplified in the May 2007 visit to the Emirates by President Ahmadinejad. Ahmadinejad announced stepped-up efforts to pry Gulf countries from their strong U.S. alliance, urging them to push out the American military from bases in the region.[48] His visit to the UAE came just days after U.S. Vice President Cheney called on Gulf nations to blunt Iran's efforts at regional dominance. In stark contrast to Cheney's low-key visit, Ahmadinejad was treated to a red-carpet welcome and greeted by federal leaders from the Emirates. But no Emirati leaders joined Ahmadinejad at his public events; there appeared to be a careful effort to keep a distance from his statements.

In three separate addresses, the Iranian leader called for American troops to "pack their bags" and leave U.S. bases in the Gulf. At a rally in a Dubai soccer stadium, an audience of several thousand reportedly chanted "Down with America!" during Ahmadinejad's speech. An Emirati analyst emphasized to the authors that the government did not endorse this rally, yet he also pointed to the delicate middle course that the UAE was attempting to chart between its American patrons, Saudi Arabia, and Iran.[49] The fact that Iran could so quickly mobilize thousands of supporters in a place like Dubai was noted with concern throughout the Gulf and especially in Saudi Arabia.[50]

Diplomatic officials in Abu Dhabi have emphasized the risks associated with an excessively close alliance with Saudi Arabia against Iran. Some of their misgivings, however, appear to focus on Riyadh's lack of

---

[47] RAND interview with a Emirati civil servant, Abu Dhabi, March 2007.

[48] "Iran's Hard-Line President Ahmadinejad Tries to Pry Gulf Arabs Out of U.S. Alliance," Associated Press, 15 May 2007.

[49] RAND interview with a UAE scholar, Abu Dhabi, May 2007.

[50] RAND interviews, Abu Dhabi and Dubai, UAE, 2007–2008.

resolve, rather than its unyielding hostility toward Iran.[51] "Most worrisome from the Emirati point of view is the position of the Saudis, who have acted like cowards so far on the nuclear issue," noted one official. "Saudi appeasement and unilateralism," this diplomat continued, "have effectively "diluted GCC efforts against Iran."[52] Another official rejected the concept of placing the UAE under a Saudi nuclear umbrella if sufficient security guarantees were not forthcoming from the United States, but argued that subsidizing an Egyptian nuclear program might be an option.

Internal divisions among the member emirates, trading ties with Iran, the islands dispute, and suspicion of Saudi Arabia have all contributed to the UAE pursuing an approach toward Iran that, while appropriately defensive, is perhaps more balanced than Riyadh would prefer.

Iraq Is a Wellspring of Bilateral Tension Affecting the Broader Gulf

As we noted in Chapter Two, the status of Iraq has been a factor that can tip Saudi-Iranian relations toward either greater animosity or cooperation. Currently, both countries recognize that what happens in Iraq in the near future will irrevocably change the political and economic landscape of the Gulf. Thus, each state perceives the struggle for Iraq as a zero-sum game.[53] This competitive view has further increased tensions within the GCC, as Gulf states attempt to formulate their policies toward Saudi Arabia, Iran, Iraq, and the United States.

---

[51] Like Oman, the UAE's posture is informed by its history of territorial tensions with Saudi Arabia, particularly over the disputed Buraymi Oasis.

[52] RAND interview with a foreign ministry official, Abu Dhabi, UAE, February 2006.

[53] "Al-Sira' al-Ta'ifi fi al-Iraq wa al-Mintaqah [The Sectarian Conflict in Iraq and the Region]," al-Jazeera Television Network, "Bila Hudud" [Without Boarders] Program, aired 20 January 2007; Mamoun Fandy, "al-'Iraq: Ja'izat al-'Arab al-Kubra [Iraq: The Great Arab Prize]," al-Sharq al-Awsat, 9 June 2008. Fandy writes that "a non-nuclear Iran uses Iraq as a platform for its influence and dominance in Lebanon, Gaza, Yemen, Bahrain, Kuwait and other Gulf countries."

Future Saudi-Iranian Involvement in Iraq Will Hinge Upon Iraq's Future Trajectory

Saudi Arabia's posture has only recently shifted from one of paralysis on Iraq and passive dismay at Iran's activism there to a more proactive engagement. Deliberations about a U.S. drawdown in Iraq have accelerated what appears to be a growing trend of introspection and self-criticism among commentators in Saudi Arabia and the broader Gulf, with many arguing that the tradition of Arab inaction on Iraq has created a power vacuum that Iran will increasingly fill after the departure of U.S. forces.[54] As of October 2008, several editorials in the Saudi press appeared to hint at a shift in Saudi Arabia's willingness to open an embassy in Baghdad, with the editor of *al-Hayat* and the general director of the Saudi-owned TV satellite channel *al-Arabiya* arguing that the Maliki government was deserving of broad Arab support.[55] According to one Sharjah-based commentator:

> The Gulf states may continue to lament the fact that Iran is interfering in the internal issues of Iraq as they persist with their policy of two steps forward, two steps back. In fact, it is only natural that Iran steps up to assume a role in its western neighbour that is at risk of falling apart to its detriment. The GCC countries must immediately awaken from their state of suspended animation.[56]

In the event of a substantive U.S. withdrawal from Iraq, Saudi-Iranian relations may evolve in drastically different directions. Much of this depends on the future trajectory of the state. A fractured polity in which the central government's control of military power has devolved to contending factions controlling substantial blocs of territory will

---

[54] Tariq al-Humayd, "al-Insihab al-Amriki al-Sakut al-Thani [The American Withdrawal: The Second Defeat]," *al-Sharq al-Awsat*, 9 October 2007. See also 'Abd al-Munim Sa'id, "al-Kharuj al-Amriki min al-'Iraq! [The American Withdrawal from Iraq]," *al-Sharq al-Awsat*, January 18, 2008.

[55] *Al-Arabiya*, 6 October; *al-Hayat*, 6 October 2008; Abd al-Rahman al-Rasheed, "Khiyar Iraq: Namuthij Iran um al-Khalij [Iraq's Choice: The Model of Iran or the Gulf]," *al-Sharq al-Awsat*, 19 February 2009.

[56] Sultan al-Qassemi, "Gulf States May Continue to Ignore Iraq at Their Own Peril," *The National* (U.A.E.) June 21, 2008.

almost certainly invite increased Saudi and Iranian interference. At the other end of the spectrum, an authoritarian, Shi'a-dominated state with a politicized military that persecutes Sunnis will almost certainly invite Saudi suspicions of Iranian influence and control. It is important to note here that Riyadh is probably resigned to living with a Shi'a-controlled government but wants it to be one that is relatively nationalistic in orientation, free from Iranian influence, inclusive of Sunnis, and unable to threaten its neighbors with reconstituted power projection.

Iran's ability and willingness to back armed factions via the Islamic Revolutionary Guards Corps–Qods Force is well understood; the Saudi capacity is less evident, although there is a clear historical precedent for indirect Saudi interference in civil conflicts, whether by funding tribal elements or encouraging Arab foreign volunteers. Aside from the most commonly cited example of Afghanistan, Riyadh was an active player in the internecine conflicts of its neighbors to the south: backing anti-Egyptian, royalist troops in the Yemeni civil war of 1962–1970; supporting the Dhofar Liberation Front in starting the Dhofar Rebellion in Oman from 1962 to 1970; and backing southern Yemen during the 1994 civil war. It should be noted that neither Iran nor Saudi Arabia has an interest in seeing Iraq devolve into total chaos, but a protracted, low-intensity proxy conflict might be seen as presenting minimal risks for each side.

As early as November–December 2006, there were several reports and testimonies that hinted that the Saudis were willing to intervene in Iraq, especially given the impending withdrawal of U.S. forces from the country. Jamal Kashoggi, who previously advised the former Saudi Ambassador to the United States, Prince Turki al-Faysal, implied that a civil war in Iraq could inspire Saudis to fight "shoulder to shoulder with al-Qaeda."[57] Nawaf Obaid, then adviser to the Saudi government, also argued that Saudi Arabia would intervene in Iraq if the United States withdrew from the country, in order to protect the Sunni population.[58]

---

[57] Jay Solomon, "Religious Divide: To Contain Iran, U.S. Seeks Help from Arab Allies," *The Wall Street Journal,* 24 November 2006.

[58] Obaid (2006b).

Finally, the Iraq Study Group Report concisely mentioned current but private Saudi involvement in the funding of the Sunni insurgency in Iraq.[59] RAND's Saudi diplomatic and think-tank interlocutors did not see the situation in Iraq escalating into a proxy war again Iran, but argued that Riyadh "could easily" support Iraqi Sunni tribes against Iranian militias and paramilitaries, using Jordan and the Shammar tribe as the principle conduits. Other contacts claimed personal knowledge that such support was already underway, with major Iraqi tribal shaykhs visiting Riyadh and being escorted back to the border with suitcases of cash.[60]

In contrast to the scenario of a breakdown in Iraq and hostile Saudi-Iranian intervention, a stable Iraq dominated by a Shi'a-led government might produce some sort of condominium arrangement between the two states. In this trajectory, Riyadh would offer tacit, if grudging, recognition of the Iraqi regime, accept a degree of Iranian influence, and continue to quietly expand its soft-power influence via media, charitable organizations, patronage of tribes, and other means. Riyadh certainly has a history of appeasing or bandwagoning with regional ideological competitors; faced with the rising tide of Nasserism in the late 1950s, for example, it refused to renew the U.S. lease on the Dhahran airfield in 1961 as a symbolic capitulation to the Egyptian president.

In Iraq, much will depend upon Saudi Arabia's perception of its loss in net power in the region *relative to Iran's gains* following a U.S. withdrawal and also the degree to which Iranian influence in Iraq is perceived to present a domestic threat to the legitimacy of the Saudi regime. Yet in the current climate, even the most pragmatic or accommodationist voices inside Saudi policy circles may be confronted with intensified domestic opposition from hard-liners in the royal family and the Salafi establishment, particularly if the regime is seen as having "lost Iraq" to Iran.

---

[59] James A. Baker III et al., *The Iraq Study Group Report: The Way Forward—A New Approach*, authorized ed., New York: Vintage Books, 2006.

[60] RAND discussions with Saudi scholars in Jeddah, March 2007.

Iran Criticizes the Saudi Role in Iraq, Particularly Riyadh's Cooperation with the United States

As noted earlier, many Iranian voices from across the factional spectrum suspect that Saudi Arabia is a proxy for U.S. regional policies and is actively undermining the Shi'a government in Iraq—despite the fact that the United States openly supports the Iraqi government. Hostile Iranian attitudes regarding the Saudi role in Iraq are expressed by reformist, conservative, and radical factions, with the radical faction associated with President Ahmadinejad taking the hardest line.

At the same time, official and semi-official Iranian media outlets—such as the Islamic Republic News Agency, Fars News, and Mehr News—typically portray the Saudi role in Iraq in a positive manner and play down suggestions of tensions between Iran and its Arab neighbors, especially Saudi Arabia. Addressing reports that Arab states, including Saudi Arabia, plan to increase their diplomatic presence in Baghdad in order to curtail Iranian power, Fars News quoted Hashem Yousef, a senior official of the Arab League, as saying, "The efforts of Arab countries in Iraq are only meant to protect the interests of Iraq and the Arab world . . . and are not due to U.S. requests or a need to confront Iran in Iraq."[61]

In an effort to shed light on the return of Saudi diplomats to Iraq, Mehr News, a media source closely associated with the Iranian government, quoted the Saudi Foreign Minister as saying, "The reasons for the absence of a Saudi embassy in Iraq are due to security issues and are not political in nature."[62] Mehr News did not mention that the absence of the Saudi embassy may be linked to the Saudi government's opposition to the Shi'a-dominated Iraqi government.

Reports and opinion editorials published by Iran's various factions have tended to treat the issue differently. According to Tabnak, a Web site closely associated with Mohsen Rezai, former commander-

---

[61] "Ezam heyethay e namayandegi Arab beh Aragh, baraye rouyarouyi ba Iran nist [The Dispatch of Arab Diplomats to Iraq Is Not Meant to Confront Iran]," Fars News Agency, 28 April 2008.

[62] "Adm bazgashti sefarat Arabistan dar Aragh be masael amniyati bar migardad [The Return of the Saudi Embassy to Iraq Will Be Determined by Security Conditions]," Mehr News Agency, 28 April 2008.

in-chief of the Islamic Revolutionary Guards Corps and current Secretary of the Expediency Council, Saudi Arabia agreed to reestablish its embassy in Baghdad on the condition that the Iraqi government would attack the Sadrist militias. In addition, Tabnak claims that the Saudi offer to Iraq was made through U.S. Secretary of State Condoleezza Rice, and followed by General Petraeus's 2008 visit to Saudi Arabia, during which he reportedly asked the Saudis to increase their presence in Iraq in order to counter Iran's influence.[63]

Another report by Tabnak recounts a conversation between the Saudi Foreign Minister, Saud al-Faysal, and Iranian Foreign Minister Manouchehr Mottaki during the April 2008 meeting of Iraq's neighbors in Kuwait. According to this report, al-Faysal asked Mottaki, "What is the level of your interference in Basra?" to which Mottaki replied, "Not as much as your interference." Furthermore, Tabnak cited Iran's alleged role in ending the April 2008 fighting in Basra, while claiming that the fighting was a result of the Saudi condition for the reestablishment of its Baghdad embassy.[64]

Other Iranian factions have taken a similarly grim view of the Saudi role in Iraq. In an article published by the reformist Entekhab News in 2007, Saudi Arabia is accused of undermining the Shi'a-dominated Maliki government. Entekhab cites an interview with Abd al-Aziz al-Hakim, the head of the Islamic Supreme Council of Iraq, in which he discusses a plot by the "intelligence agencies of regional states to overthrow the Iraqi government headed by Nuri al-Maliki."[65]

---

[63] "Shart ajib e Saudiha baraye bazgashti sefarat dar Baghdad [The Saudis' Strange Condition for the Return of Their Embassy to Baghdad]," Tabnak News, 9 April 2008. Tabnak, which follows the format of a political blog rather than a news site, is considered by many Iranians to be the mouthpiece of the Rezai-led faction of the "pragmatist conservatives." Tabnak was formerly named Batzab.com, but it was renamed after it was momentarily closed down.

[64] "Moshajreh Mottaki va Saud Al Faisal dar hashiye neshast Kuwait [Discussions between Mottaki and Saud al-Faisal on the Margins of the Kuwait Meeting]," Tabnak News, 28 April 2008.

[65] Entekhab News, "Tavafogh sazmanhaye etelaati keshvarhay e mantaghe jahat brandazi dolat Aragh khbar dad [Agreement Among Regional Countries' Intelligence Agencies to Overthrow Maliki Government]," 12 July 2007.

Although Hakim does not mention Saudi Arabia by name, his interview followed a July 2007 meeting of GCC states in Riyadh, during which the participants discussed the security situation in Iraq. The meeting was unusual in that it included the intelligence directors of each GCC country.[66]

The radical Web site Raja News, closely associated with President Ahmadinejad, has made even stronger accusations against Saudi Arabia. In one report, Raja News claims that the Bush Administration, exhausted by the Iraq war and concerned about the prospects of the Republican Party in the 2008 U.S. presidential elections, planned to "share" its burdens in Iraq with Saudi Arabia.[67] According to this account, Iran is the primary target for this burden-sharing plan, which was conceived during visits by U.S. Vice President Dick Cheney, General Petraeus, and U.S. Ambassador to Saudi Arabia Ryan Crocker. The report also claims that the April 2008 conference of Iraq's neighbors in Kuwait and meetings between Secretary Rice with Arab officials is "the beginning of a new period of regional crisis brought about with Saudi participation."[68]

To counter U.S.-Saudi collusion in Iraq, Iran has repeated its calls for an indigenous regional security framework that would exclude external actors. Ahmadinejad himself made overtures in this direction throughout spring and summer of 2007, extending an invitation to Saudi Arabia to cooperate with Iran in "filling the vacuum" left by departing U.S. forces. The Saudi response was muted, yet critical. One editorial in *al-Sharq al-Awsat* rejected Iran's logic of "vacuum filling," comparing it to America's assumption of British imperial rule after the announcement of Britain's "east of Suez" withdrawal.[69] This criticism illustrates that, even when Riyadh fears that the United States may withdraw from the region, it chooses to strengthen its independent

---

[66] Raid Qusti, "GCC to Confront Iraq Security Fallout," *Arab News*, 4 July 2007.

[67] "Mamuriat e jadid e America bray e Arabistan, Mesr, va Ordon [America's New Instructions for Saudi Arabia. Egypt, and Jordan]," Raja News, 24 April 2008.

[68] "Mamuriat e jadid e America" (2008).

[69] Bilal al-Hasan: "Ahmadinejad's Grave Mistake: The Theory of Vacuum Filling," *al-Sharq al-Awsat* (in Arabic), 2 September 2007.

position rather than to accept a junior role within an Iranian-led security framework.

The Nuclear Issue Has Spurred Tension, but also Mutual Threat Management

Aside from Iraq, Iran's nuclear ambitions remain the other key issue of contention affecting Saudi and Iranian posture toward the Gulf. Each has sought to solicit regional support for its claims on this issue. Although the prospect of a nuclear Iran has been interpreted in some Saudi quarters as an existential threat to the Kingdom, Saudi policy has been more nuanced than expected. Saudi Arabia and its Gulf neighbors have performed a delicate balancing act in their policies toward Iran, seeking to manage the nuclear threat through accommodation rather than confrontation, publicly voicing their disapproval of a U.S. strike, and making calls for WMD-free zone in the Gulf and the Middle East. For its part, Tehran recognizes that its nuclear energy ambitions must be accompanied by careful perception-management efforts toward its Gulf neighbors.

Saudi Nuclear Fears Are Balanced by a Range of Other Concerns

Iran's nuclear ambition is one issue on which Saudi thinking is closer to Europe than the United States. Despite profound worries over Tehran's nuclear ambitions, Riyadh's key decisionmakers appear convinced that tacit cooperation is superior to confrontation and threats—principally because they fear the chaos of a U.S. strike more than the effects of Iran's nuclear acquisition. They are also likely to perceive significant GCC divisions over the threat perceived by a nuclear Iran and how best to proceed.[70]

---

[70] These insights are derived from the author's interviews in Oman, the UAE, Kuwait, Bahrain, and Saudi Arabia during February 2006, November 2006, and March 2007. For more on Gulf and regional perceptions of the nuclear impasse, see Kaye and Wehrey (2007), Karim Sadjadpour, "The Nuclear Players," *Journal of International Affairs*, Vol. 60, No. 2, Spring/Summer 2007; Richard L. Russell, "Peering Over the Horizon: Arab Threat Perception and Security Responses to a Nuclear-Ready Iran," Non-Proliferation Policy Education Center, 5 February 2005; Judith S. Yaphe and Charles D. Lutes, *Reassessing the Implications*

In attempting to emphasize their concerns about Iran, Riyadh and other Gulf Arab regimes are engaged in a delicate balancing act. They are ultimately wary that Arab audiences may interpret their opposition to Iran's nuclear ambitions as an implicit endorsement of a U.S. military strike—which they know would damage both their regional and domestic standing. One remedy to this dilemma, therefore, is to publicly argue against a U.S. strike, make vague and somewhat anemic calls for "dialogue" with Iran on the nuclear issue, and to shift the public debate to Israel by proposing a nuclear-free zone in the Middle East that would include Tel Aviv's abandonment of its own undeclared capability.[71] For example, in an interview with *al-Hayat* on June 22, 2007, the Saudi Foreign Minister warned against the dangers of using force against Iran and stressed "the need to turn the Middle East into a nuclear-free zone."[72]

One of the questions that Gulf states—and Saudi Arabia in particular—have had to ask is the extent to which a nuclear Iran would change the strategic climate in the Gulf. Although Saudi Arabia's decision to join the Nuclear Non-Proliferation Treaty (NPT) in 1988 was political rather than strategic, there is the real possibility that the Saudis will indeed pursue their own weapons program.[73] Thus far, the United States' security guarantees to Saudi Arabia have represented a funda-

---

of a Nuclear-Armed Iran, McNair Paper 69, Washington, D.C.: National Defense University, 2005; Simon Henderson, "The Elephant in the Gulf: The Arab States and Iran's Nuclear Program," Washington Institute for Near East Policy, Policy Watch 1065, 21 December 2005; and "Analysis: Arab Dilemma Over Iran's Nuclear Program," BBC Monitoring, translated by Open Source Center, FEA20070627206546, 27 June 2007.

[71] RAND interviews with foreign ministry officials, journalists, and military commanders in the UAE, Kuwait, and Oman in March 2006 and July 2007. See also "Kayfa Yandhuru al-Arab ila Iran? [Panorama: How Do Arabs View Iran?]," *al-Arabia Television Network*, Panorama program, 26 February 2007; and Abd al-Rahman al-Rashid, "Li hathihi al-Asbab Naksha Iran [For These Reasons We Fear Iran]," *Al-Sharq Al-Awsat*, 18 April 2006.

[72] "UK Daily Views Gulf Arabs' Dilemma Over Response to Iran's Suspected Ambitions" (2007).

[73] Thomas Lippman, "Saudi Arabia: The Calculations of Uncertainty," *The Nuclear Tipping Point*, Brookings Institution Press, 2004.

mental incentive for the Kingdom to curb its own nuclear programs.[74] Saudi officials realize that any change in their nuclear policy would lead the West and especially the United States to give Saudi Arabia the same treatment it has given Iran and North Korea. But with a second, more conservative, generation of Saudi princes rising in the al-Saud power circles, there may be cause for concern.[75]

Much will depend on how Iran crosses the nuclear threshold—transparently, opaquely, or using a more subtle form of "calculated ambiguity." The latter two will reduce significantly the security dilemma for Arab regimes, giving them a fig leaf to avoid more drastic changes in their security posture. From Tehran's perspective, there may be voices that argue for this route to preserve Iran's standing in the Gulf and avoid pushing Gulf states deeper into the embrace of the United States. The disadvantage, of course, is that a nontransparent route denies Iran the domestic benefit of prestige that an open test would afford.

In September 2003, the *Guardian* reported that Saudi Arabia had launched a strategic security review that included the possible acquisition of nuclear weapons. According to the *Guardian* report, the strategy paper being considered at the highest levels in Riyadh sets out three options:

- to acquire a nuclear capability as a deterrent
- to maintain or enter into an alliance with an existing nuclear power that would offer protection
- to try to reach a regional agreement on having a nuclear-free Middle East.[76]

In December 2006, GCC Secretary General Abd al-Rahman al-Attiyah announced the GCC states' intention to establish a joint

---

[74] Gawdat Bahgat, "Nuclear Proliferation: The Case of Saudi Arabia," *Middle East Journal*, Vol. 60, No. 3, Summer 2006.

[75] RAND interviews with Saudi officials and media representatives, Dubai and Abu Dhabi, UAE, November 2007.

[76] Ewen MacAskill and Ian Traynor, "Saudis Consider Nuclear Bomb," *The Guardian*, 18 September 2003.

nuclear research program. The decision was significant because it indicated to Iran that the Gulf states, which had a long history of rejecting any nuclear energy activity, were leaving their options open to develop a military program.[77] The UAE, Bahrain, and Kuwait went even further and decided to begin bilateral negotiations with the International Atomic Energy Agency (IAEA) to consider the establishment of their own separate civilian nuclear programs. This action sent a twofold message: first, that these states' programs were not linked to Saudi Arabia, and second, that they would never be part of the Iranian nuclear energy effort.[78]

Iranian Sources Downplay Saudi Threat Perception of the Nuclear Program

From Iran's point of view, Saudi Arabia's nonconfrontational approach to the nuclear issue provides a welcome public relations opportunity. Iranian sources often portray Saudi Arabia as accepting the "peaceful" nature of Iran's nuclear program. In addition, Saudi Arabia is repeatedly shown to be concerned about U.S. strikes on Iran's nuclear facilities.

Iran's newest broadcast agency, the English language Press TV, quoted Saud al-Faysal: "Iran is not a threat . . . we have expressed our hope that the Iranian crisis in solved peacefully."[79] In addition, Fars News reported that "Riyadh Backs Iran Nuclear Program" and quoted King Abdullah saying that "all countries have a right to peaceful use of nuclear energy in accord with the norms of the International Atomic Energy Agency" and, in a "thinly veiled reference to the Zionist regime," reported him saying that "the criterion (should) be applied to all countries in the region without exception."[80] Tabnak reported that a recent poll conducted in Arab countries indicated that 73 percent of Saudis "support" the Iranian nuclear program. Saudi "support"

---

[77] Nicole Stracke, "Nuclear Development in the Gulf: A Strategic or Economic Necessity," *Security and Terrorism Research Bulletin*, Gulf Research Center, No. 7, December 2007, p. 4.

[78] Stracke (2007).

[79] "Saudis Say Iran No Threat," Press TV, 7 July 2007.

[80] "Riyadh Backs Iran N. Program," Fars News Agency, 20 June 2007.

for the nuclear program reportedly surpassed such "support" in other Arab countries.[81]

However, this is not to suggest that Iranians believe that the nuclear issue is free from tension. Responding to Saudi and French demands that Iran adhere to the framework of the NPT, Iran's Foreign Ministry spokesman, Mohammad Ali Hosseini, stated that "Iran supports a Middle East free of nuclear weapons" and that its program was "peaceful and under the supervision of the IAEA." Furthermore, Hosseini stated, "We hope that our Saudi friends are not influenced by the satanic temptations of extra-regional powers."[82]

Saudi Arabia is also shown in the Iranian press to fear a potential military conflict between Iran and the United States. According to Tabnak and other sources, Saudi King Abdullah, in his March 2008 discussion with U.S. Vice President Dick Cheney, rejected "any sort of military attacks on Iran" and viewed "negotiations as the best way to reduce tensions between Iran and the U.S."[83]

Although Saudi Arabia and its Gulf Arab neighbors have serious concerns about Iran's nuclear intentions, even bringing Saudi Arabia to the point of considering whether to acquire its own nuclear deterrent, Saudi Arabia and Iran have maintained an outward tone of cooperation in the interest of threat management. Each side has its particular motives for maintaining this approach, with Iran enjoying the cover of Saudi "approval" and Saudi Arabia seeking to avoid the fallout of a U.S. military action. Yet such pragmatism has so far worked to keep tensions manageable.

---

[81] "Taghier negrash nesbat beh barbame atomi Iran Iran [A change in the level of anxiety among Arabs regarding Iran's nuclear program]," *Tabnak.ir*, 15 April 2008. Other Arab countries polled included Jordan, Lebanon, the UAE, Morocco, and Egypt.

[82] Entekhab News, "Vaknesh Hosseini beh bayaniyeh Arabestan va France [Hosseini's Reaction to French and Saudi Statements]," 17 January 2008.

[83] "Mokhalafat Arabistan ba eghdam nezami alayhe Iran [Saudi Arabia's Opposition to Military Attacks Against Iran]," 17 January 2008.

Differences over Oil and Gas Are Sources of Further Contention

Despite examples of cooperation and threat management, there are some areas where Saudi Arabia and Iran have competed. Oil is one such area, with obvious importance to the entire Gulf region. Time is an important source of tension between the two countries. Iran is more concerned about the short-term future of world oil markets, while the Saudis focus more on the long term. This difference in temporal priorities is due to trends in oil reserves and production capacity. Recent analysis indicates that Iran has 136 billion barrels of oil reserves, while Saudi Arabia hosts 267 billion barrels of reserves.[84] Also, forecasts from the World Energy Outlook suggest that Saudi Arabia's output will climb from 10.2 mb/d (million barrels per day) in 2007 to 14.4 mb/d in 2015 and 15.6 mb/d in 2030. In contrast, Iran's production may be shrinking by as much as 10 to 15 percent per year due to its deteriorating oil infrastructure, government mismanagement and a skyrocketing growth in domestic demand driven by subsidies.[85] Production costs in each country also influence energy outlook; the cost of extracting a barrel of oil in Saudi Arabia is reportedly $2 to $3 a barrel, one of the lowest in the world, whereas in Iran the cost is roughly $15 dollar a barrel because of Iran's bloated and inefficient oil sector.[86]

Clearly, Iran is interested in maximizing oil profits in the near term while its position in the market is relatively strong; the Saudis have an incentive to moderate prices for now to mitigate the challenge from non-OPEC producers and ensure that developed nations do not

---

[84] U.S. Department of Energy, Energy Information Administration, Country Analysis Briefs, Saudi Arabia and Iran, August 2008.

[85] International Energy Agency, "World Energy Outlook, 2008." Iran's domestic oil demand grew by 6 percent in 2007, the largest in the world. In 2007, Iran's representative to OPEC admitted the deleterious effects of this consumption on Iran's oil industry. "Iran Admits Hurt by High Domestic Oil Consumption," Agence France Presse, 9 September 2007.

[86] This is also because Iran has limited refining capacity and must import 40 percent of its gasoline. Robert Windrem, "Are Saudis Waging an Oil-Price War on Iran?" *MSNBC*, January 26, 2007.

begin a major push toward alternative energy sources.[87] Iran also has a demographic reason for a near-term focus that would bring it into conflict with the Saudis in OPEC; the Iranian youth bulge will be cresting in the next decade, and high oil revenues in the short term help Tehran buy off the increasingly frustrated youth population with subsidies.[88]

A second aspect of this energy competition is the future oil policy of Iraq, which has 115 billion barrels of proven oil reserves—the second largest in the world.[89] Whichever state, Iran or Saudi Arabia, has more influence in a future Iraq will gain a powerful partner in OPEC deliberations, in addition to the other strategic and ideological benefits that influence in Iraq would bring. This economic motivation could be expected to heighten the two countries' level of competition over Iraq.[90]

A third source of friction involves the nature of foreign investment in Iran and its geopolitical consequences. Iran's energy infrastructure is in disrepair, and, since Western firms still face U.S. sanctions should they invest in Iran, there is a strong chance that Russian firms might fill this vacuum. Russia has a keen interest in seeing Iran's oil profits sustained because this gives Iran the foreign exchange it needs to purchase advanced Russian conventional weapons, thus keeping the Russian defense industry capable and viable. A strong Russian-Iranian oil partnership would strengthen the already developing political-military

---

[87] In March 2008, there were reports that Saudi cuts in production came at the behest of U.S. Vice President Cheney during his visit to Riyadh and were explicitly targeted at Iran. "Latent Saudi-Iran Oil Price War Seen," APS Diplomatic News Service, 24 March 2008.

[88] For more on Iran's demographic and energy challenges, see Keith Crane, Rollie Lal, Jeffrey Martini, *Iran's Political, Demographic, and Economic Vulnerabilities*, Santa Monica, Calif.: RAND, 2008.

[89] U.S. Department of Energy, Energy Information Administration, Country Analysis Briefs, Iraq, 2008. Iraqi Deputy Prime Minister Barham Salih claimed in mid-2008 that the country had 350 billion barrels, making it the largest in the world. Sonia Verma, "Iraq Could Have Largest Oil Reserves in the World," *The Times* (UK), 20 May 2008.

[90] Research Institute of Strategic Studies, "Bohran-e Aragh va payamadhaye manfiye an bar amniyat va manafe melli jomhouriye eslamiye Iran [Iraq's Crisis and Its Negative Consequences on Iran's Security and National Interests]," 2003.

links between the two states, intensifying Saudi concern about Iran's ambitions and power-projection capabilities in the Gulf.[91]

Aside from oil, natural gas (and liquefied natural gas, or LNG, in its transportation form) is a growing and future concern that challenges Saudi policy in the Gulf and benefits Iran, whether an OPEC-like gas cartel is formed or not. Of course, Qatar is the major player within the Gulf for gas energy, but gas networks such as Dolphin or Dana make the UAE and Oman stakeholders as well. Qatar appears to using the Dolphin project to bolster political ties to Oman and the UAE in order to counterbalance Saudi Arabia.[92] The key question now is the degree to which the formation of a gas cartel similar to OPEC will affect Saudi-Iranian relations.

On January 29, 2007, Iranian Supreme Leader Ayatollah Ali Khamenei stated that Iran and Russia should create an export group like OPEC, based on their command of the world's largest reserves of natural gas.[93] The reaction from Saudi Arabia was muted, but behind-the-scenes discussions with Qatar about the prospects for such a cartel and the impact upon the region were discussed at the highest levels.[94] In late October 2008, energy officials from Russia, Qatar, and Iran announced further deliberations on the cartel, marking the most substantive meeting on the issue since Khamenei's announcement.[95] Overall, however, the prospects seem bleak for any OPEC-like body; unlike oil, gas supply deals are fixed on long-term contracts, making

---

[91] In July 2008, Russia's Gaziprom signed a deal to develop Iran's South Pars gas field and oil projects in the Caspian and Azadegan region.

[92] See Justin Dargin, "Qatar's Natural Gas: The Foreign Policy Driver," *Middle East Policy*, Vol. 14, No. 3, fall 2007, pp. 136–147.

[93] The idea for the gas organization arose with the signing of an alliance between the Russian gas company Gazprom and the Algerian company Sonatrach in 2006, two of the major suppliers of natural gas to Europe. Since then, the Iranian Ayatollah Ali Khamenei proposed the idea to the Russian President Vladimir Putin, who considered the idea "interesting" and expressed his support for some sort of organization between producers. Soon after, Venezuelan President Hugo Chávez also expressed interest.

[94] RAND interviews in Qatar and the UAE, November and December 2007.

[95] "Iran, Russia, Qatar Mull Forming OPEC-Style Natural Gas Cartel," Associated Press, 21 October 2008.

short-term price manipulation difficult. These limitations will likely leave Iran to coordinate gas policy with Russia and Saudi Arabia, and the Gulf states to continue to carry out their own various national projects.

Conclusion

Outside of ideology and the character of their respective regimes, Saudi Arabia and Iran would appear structurally inclined toward rivalry in the Gulf. Resources and geography are potential sources of contention exacerbated by Iran's new nationalism and the continuing problem of Shi'a marginalization in Bahrain and Saudi Arabia. Iran's active role in Iraq, its nuclear ambitions, and its energy differences with Saudi Arabia are further flashpoints that complicate the bilateral relationship.

That said, this chapter has also shown how diversity and disunity within the GCC pose challenges for both Riyadh and Tehran, with the ultimate effect of tempering their rivalry. The economic resources of the region, coupled with each state's increasingly proactive foreign policies, also make the Gulf a valuable bridge between Saudi Arabia and Iran for pursuing cooperation. Pragmatic currents inside Riyadh and Tehran recognize the value of working within this context to bring stability to the Gulf littoral while juggling security and economic priorities. For U.S. policymakers, it is important to note how these economic partnerships are a way of reinforcing Tehran's stake in regional stability.

Much of the wary engagement and pragmatism that defines relations in the Gulf is rooted in the simple fact of physical proximity. In more removed regions, such as the Levant, Tehran can afford to pursue policies that are more belligerent and radical. This, in turn, has prompted a more concerted response of rollback from Saudi Arabia. We examine the unfolding of bilateral rivalry in this peripheral area in the next chapter.

CHAPTER FOUR

Contention on the Periphery: Saudi-Iranian Relations and the Conflicts in Lebanon and Palestine

If Saudi-Iranian relations within the immediate neighborhood of the Gulf are defined by conflict regulation and muted rivalry, the two states have pursued more open competition in the Levant. Much of the difference between the Gulf and Levantine landscapes stems from Iran's bifurcated policy in the region: Although it abandoned its support of militancy on the Arabian Peninsula in the mid-1990s, its assertiveness and patronage of nonstate actors has continued largely unabated in Lebanon and in Palestine. Moreover, the Levantine arena contains no natural resources that can temper the rivalry. Finally, the fractured nature of these states and their weak governments have historically invited outside meddling.

Both Riyadh and Tehran recognize that the symbolic stakes of the conflict in Palestine and the political struggle in Lebanon are enormous, as demonstrated by the ongoing fighting in Gaza and the 2006 Lebanon War. The Israeli-Palestinian issue taps into Arab public opinion well beyond the Levant and, as we have mentioned, Iran sees the exploitation of this sentiment as a way to undercut unfriendly Arab regimes. Lebanon is considered a prize for historical, political, and commercial reasons. Iran has made substantial political and military commitments to the country since the Revolution, and Saudi Arabia has stepped up its involvement since the assassination of Prime Minister Rafik Hariri, a longtime ally of Riyadh. Syria has also been an object of contention because it acts as Iran's conduit into Levantine affairs.

Saudi diplomacy since 2005 has been focused on wrestling Syria from Tehran's orbit to bring it back to the Arab fold and, short of this, keeping it isolated and weak.

Despite these sources of competition, Saudi Arabia and Iran have frequently deemed it advantageous to manage their rivalry in ways that avoid the escalation of conflict and, in the case of Lebanon, that even involve sporadic diplomatic coordination. This chapter will discuss the ebb and flow of these dynamics.

Developments in Lebanon Have Stimulated Competition, but Riyadh and Tehran Have Avoided Open Conflict

Saudi Arabia and Iran have significant, long-standing interests in Lebanon. Clerical relations between Lebanon and Iran pre-date the Revolution, and Hizballah's zone of control in southern Beirut arguably represents the most compelling example of Iranian near-success in exporting the Revolution. Saudi Arabia, for its part, has long seen Lebanon as a proxy arena to outmaneuver its regional competitors, illustrated by its support in the 1950s and 60s to Lebanese opponents of Nasserism such as Pierre Gemayyel and Kamil Sham'un. Lebanon also proved immensely important for Saudi Arabia to raise its leadership profile on the pan-Arab stage after Egypt's effective abandonment of its role with the signing of the Camp David Accords; Riyadh successfully hosted the Taif Accords, which ended the Lebanese Civil War. In the religious sphere, Saudi Arabia has been a long-standing patron of Salafi currents in the country's Palestinian camps and cities such as Sidon and Tripoli.[1]

---

[1] For background, see As'ad AbuKhalil, "Determinants and Characteristics of the Saudi Role in Lebanon: The Post-Civil War Years," in Madawi al-Rasheed, ed., *Kingdom Without Borders: Saudi Arabia's Political, Religious and Media Frontiers*, London: Hurst and Company, 2008, pp. 79–97. Also see Amal Saad-Ghorayeb, *Hizbu'llah: Politics and Religion*, Sterling, Va.: Pluto Press, 2002. A Salafi cleric in Tripoli opined to RAND that Salafism had difficulty taking root in Lebanon; most Lebanese Sunnis followed the Hanafi *madhhab* (Islamic legal school) and were too lax in their social mores. "Everybody here wants to eat kebab and visit the cedars," this cleric lamented. RAND interview in Abu Samra, Tripoli, March 2008.

Two major events in recent years—the 2005 political crisis following the assassination of former Lebanese Prime Minister Rafik Hariri and the subsequent "Cedar Revolution," and the 2006 war between Israel and Hizballah—emerged as the central catalysts for increased intervention by each side.[2]

The 2005 Political Crisis Forced a Choice Between Conflict and Cooperation

Since the assassination of Hariri in February 2005, Lebanon's domestic political struggle has represented an opportunity for Iran and Saudi Arabia to test each other's intentions and goals in that country. The assassination stirred long-dormant tensions between two rival coalitions and respective allies of Tehran and Riyadh. While Iran and Syria have supported the March 8 Alliance—which includes Hizballah, Amal, and Michel Aoun's Free Patriotic Movement—Saudi Arabia found a natural ally in the rival pro-Hariri coalition, the "March 14 Alliance."[3] The face-off between the March 8 and March 14 Alliances is often considered as a surrogate confrontation between Iran and Saudi Arabia. Several interlocutors, however, noted that external involvement is often used as a convenient pretext by local factions to avoid any compromise. "You can't be seen as giving in here, unless your outside patron tells you," one analyst argued. "This gives you the fig leaf of cover. Here, there is the sense that Lebanon's future will be decided in Damascus, Riyadh, and Tehran."[4]

---

[2] The Cedar Revolution was a chain of demonstrations in Lebanon triggered by the Hariri assassination. The primary goals of the original activists were the withdrawal of Syrian troops from Lebanon, the replacement of the Syrian influence with a patriotic Lebanese government, the establishment of an international commission to investigate the assassination of Hariri, the resignation of security officials to ensure the success of the plan, and the organization of free parliamentary elections.

[3] The March 14 Alliance is named for an anti-Syria demonstration that took place in Beirut on March 14, 2005, following the assassination of Rafik Hariri. The pro-Syria March 8 Alliance is named for a 2006 demonstration on that date thanking Syria for its prior assistance to Lebanon.

[4] RAND interview with Lebanese analyst, Beirut, February 2008.

Neither Saudi Arabia nor Iran necessarily has any interest in an open confrontation between their allies in the various confessional regions throughout Lebanon.[5] In fact, one of the immediate consequence of Saudi support to the March 14 Alliance and to its Cedar Revolution was the intensification of Riyadh's estrangement from Syria's Bashar al-Assad, considered by some to be the main culprit behind the Hariri assassination.[6] As a result, Saudi Arabia favored Iran as a negotiating partner, believing that the two states could work out a power-sharing agreement between their nonstate allies that would preserve a Saudi sphere of influence in the country and undercut Syria.[7] Conversely, factions within the Iranian regime, facing political opposition and discontent at home, saw value in reaching an accord with

---

[5]   Under Lebanon's confessional system, certain political offices are proportionately reserved for representatives from certain religious communities. At the highest level, the President is a Christian Maronite, the Prime Minister is a Sunni, and the Speaker of the Parliament is a Shi'a.

[6]   Following the assassination, Syria was forced to withdraw its troops from Lebanon. But the extent to which Damascus has truly disengaged from Lebanon is unclear, in spite of the redeployment of an estimated 16,000 Syrian troops in April 2005. As a matter of fact, after Hariri's death, a series of anti-Syrian personalities of Lebanon were killed in car bombings, including journalist Samir Kassir (June 2005) and politicians Pierre Gemayel (November 2006) and Walid Eido (May 2007). Syrian responsibility emerged after two UN reports, the Fitzgerald Report and the Mehlis Report, underscored Syria's influence in Lebanese affairs and the involvement of highly ranked Syrian officials in the Hariri's assassination. In May 2007, Resolution 1757 established a UN International Tribunal to prosecute the culprits. See Hussain Abdul-Hussain, "Standing up to Killers: Syria Must Answer for Its Murders in Lebanon," *The Washington Post*, June 14, 2007; "Report of the International Independent Investigation Commission Established Pursuant to Security Council Resolution 1595," 20 October 2005; "Last Syrian Troops Leave Lebanon," *CNN*, 27 April 2005; and "Report of the Fact-Finding Mission to Lebanon," 24 March 2005.

[7]   "Iran's FM Mottaki on Nuke File, Larijani, US Threats, Shi'a Crescent, Saudi Ties," *al-Dammam al-Yawm*, translated by Open Source Center, GMP20071126614006, 26 November 2007; Gause (2007a), Slackman (2007a, 2007b); Middle East Media Research Institute, "Recent Saudi-Iranian Contacts to Resolve the Lebanon Crisis," *Special Dispatch Series*, 26 January 2007; "Al-Manar Reports on Saudi-Iranian Talks, Initial Understanding on Lebanese File," *al-Manar Television* (Beirut), translated by Open Source Center, GMP20070126644001, 26 January 2007; Mouna Naïm, "Riyadh Solicits Damascus to Alleviate Lebanese Tensions," *Le Monde* (Paris; in French), 26 January 2007, p. 4; and Nicholas Blanford, "Is Iran Driving New Saudi Diplomacy?" *Christian Science Monitor*, 16 January 2007a.

Riyadh that would preserve the standing of Hizballah.[8] This configuration allowed the two powers to maintain a subtle relationship that went beyond mere competition.

The negotiations involve a series of closed-door diplomatic efforts and envoy visits in Tehran and in Riyadh, involving high-ranking officials, including Prince Bandar Bin Sultan, Secretary General of the Saudi National Security Council, and Ali Larijani, then Secretary of Iran's Supreme Council for National Security. Cooperation between the two powers limited the violence and enabled a power-sharing agreement in the short run.[9] Similarly, after violence broke out in January 2007 between forces of the two coalitions, Saudi Arabia actively promoted the "success" of its cooperation with Iran, in order to show that joint efforts were the key to stabilizing Lebanon and promoting overall Muslim welfare.[10] Yet this equilibrium was upset by the growth of Hizballah's bargaining power following the 2006 war with Israel and its May 2008 move in West Beirut.

Riyadh and Tehran Each Saw the 2006 War as an Opportunity to Assert Its Regional Leadership

From Riyadh's perspective, the 2006 war between Israel and Hizballah represented an almost seismic shift in the regional balance of power in Iran's favor. In the subsequent rush to provide aid in the aftermath, Saudi Arabia sent a clear message to Tehran that it intended to balance, and even roll back, Iranian influence in postwar Lebanon.[11] Riyadh blamed Hizballah (and indirectly, Iran) for triggering the war and made its commitment to the reconstruction of Lebanon a top priority.[12] The Saudi pledge amounted to $1.5 billion, with $1 billion trans-

---

[8]   RAND discussion with a European analyst, Beirut, February 2008.

[9]   This preserved, in the short run, the confessional system in Lebanon.

[10]   Jumana al-Tamimi, "Rivals Turn Up Heat on Siniora," *Gulf News*, 9 January 2007.

[11]   Gause (2007a); "Saudi Foreign Minister on Lebanon, Iraq, Sectarian Issues" (2007); Nawaf Obaid, "Regional Ramifications of the Lebanon Ceasefire: A Saudi View," *Saudi-US Relations Information Service*, 27 September 2006a.

[12]   At first, the war did not create a consensus among leaders of the Arab world against Israel. After harsh criticism, Hizballah leader Hassan Nasrallah was even forced to formulate

ferred to the Lebanese Central Bank for domestic economic support and the rest channeled through the Arab International Reconstruction Fund.[13] Additional aid for infrastructure came from the Saudi Development Fund.[14] Saudi Arabia also promoted an education initiative by paying for all Lebanese students for one year of their education.[15]

For its part, Tehran sought to capitalize on Hizballah's new-found popularity in the region, challenge Saudi leadership in the Levant, and mitigate Western support for the March 14 Alliance.[16] These goals explain Tehran's willingness to negotiate a solution in which Hizballah could maintain and develop its political position.[17] But in practice, Iran's financial commitment to the reconstruction has not been as sizable as Saudi Arabia's—according to some reports, its investment has only reached $120 million and has been focused mostly on schools,

---

regrets over the original strategy in August 2006. See "Saudi Editorial: Nasrallah's Statement Proves Saudi Stand on Lebanon War Sound," *al-Watan* (Abha), translated by Open Source Center, GMP20060829614007, 29 August 2006; "Nasrallah Interviewed on Lebanese Television," New TV Channel, Open Source Center Feature, FEA20060827026917, 27 August 2006; "Hizballah's Nasrallah Discusses Recent War, Supports Army, UNIFIL Deployment" *New TV Channel* (Beirut), GMP20060828617001, 27 August 2006; Alfred B. Prados and Christopher M. Blanchard, *Saudi Arabia: Current Issues and U.S. Relations*, CRS Report for Congress, Washington, D.C.: Congressional Research Service, 9 January 2007; and Obaid (2006a).

[13] Prados and Blanchard (2007).

[14] "Saudi Development Fund Agrees to Finance Express Road in Northern Lebanon," Saudi Press Agency (Riyadh), GMP20061016831004, 16 October 2006.

[15] Obaid (2006a).

[16] In 2006, 68 percent of populations from the UAE, Saudi Arabia, Morocco, Lebanon, Jordan, and Egypt had a more favorable opinion of Hizballah after the war. The highest approval came from Jordan (74 percent), Egypt (71 percent), and Morocco (70 percent). About a quarter of Sunnis, Christians, and Druze across the region had a more favorable opinion of the movement after the war. Hassan Nasrallah also became the most admired leader in the Arab world. See Shibley Telhami, "2008 Annual Arab Public Opinion Poll," Survey of the Anwar Sadat Chair for Peace and Development at the University of Maryland (with Zogby International), March 2008. See also Knickmeyer (2006, p. A19).

[17] "Iran's FM Mottaki on Nuke File, Larijani, US Threats, Shi'a Crescent, Saudi Ties" (2007); Slackman (2007a, 2007b); Blanford (2007a); and "Iran and Saudi Arabia Confrontation in the Middle East" (2006).

clinics, and bridges in the Shi'a environs of Beirut. In tandem, Iran has stepped up logistical and military support to Hizballah.[18]

Saudi Arabia has been countering the postwar rise of Hizballah with increased support to the country's Salafi factions, particularly those aligned with the prominent al-Shahal family. A Salafi cleric in Tripoli told RAND researchers that Saudi Arabia has traditionally seen Salafi currents in the Palestinian camps as "strategic depth" against Iranian power in Lebanon and that Lebanon's historically quietist Salafis have been spurred toward greater political activism because of Hizballah's ascendancy and Saudi financial support [19]

Saad Hariri, the son of Rafik Hariri, has played a critical role as an intermediary in this effort, by providing $52 million (much of it from Saudi Arabia) to the Sunni populations of the northern part of the country to counter the influence of Hizballah and, by extension, Iran.[20] Prominent Salafis aligned with the al-Shahal family have emerged as strong political supporters of Hariri's Future Movement, although there were indications as of late 2008 that this cooperation was souring and that Salafis were increasingly moving out of politics, toward possible re-radicalization.[21] An important secondary effect of this growing activism is increased Shi'a support for Hizballah. Several Shi'a contacts told the authors that, despite Shi'a frustration with Hizballah's sluggish progress on reconstruction, there was increasing support for the militant group "because no one else will protect us from the Salafis."[22]

Hizballah, for its part, has attempted to dilute and even accommodate the Sunni front through outreach to Saudi Arabia and by cut-

---

[18] Kitty Logan, "Iran Rebuilds Lebanon to Boost Hizbollah," *The Telegraph*, 31 July 2007.

[19] RAND discussion with a Salafi cleric, Tripoli, Lebanon, February 2008. See also "Sunni Rising: The Growth of Sunni Militancy in Lebanon," *Jane's Intelligence Review*, 5 December 2007; "Fatah al-Islam," *Jane's World Insurgency and Terrorism*, 26 June 2007; and Nicholas Blandford, "Chaos Returns to Troubled Lebanon," *Jane's Defence Weekly*, Vol. 44, No. 22, 30 May 2007b.

[20] RAND discussion with Lebanese analysts, Beirut, February 2008.

[21] RAND discussion with Salafi cleric, Tripoli, Lebanon, February 2008.

[22] RAND discussion with Shi'a activists in southern Beirut, February 2008.

ting deals with key Salafi players.[23] Hizballah politician and current Minister of Labour Muhammad Fneish travelled to Riyadh following the 2006 war and as of 2008 Hizballah had signed a memorandum of understanding with the Salafi Belief and Justice Movement, a group represented by the son of prominent Salafi cleric Da'i al-Islam al-Shahal.[24] According to one interlocutor, this outreach is driven by Hizballah's concerns that Lebanese Christians represent the more pressing strategic foe in Lebanon. "With the Sunnis," this analyst argued, "Hizballah at least shares the vocabulary of *muqawama* (resistance) and *jihad*."[25]

Saudi-Iranian Tension over Lebanon Could Worsen

Although Saudi Arabia and Iran have thus far found it prudent to wage their struggle for influence and primacy in Lebanon in muted ways, it is important to emphasize the underlying tension and suspicion at the core of both sides' positions.

In Iran, official and unofficial views of Saudi involvement in Lebanon are critical and often depict Saudi Arabia as interfering in Lebanese affairs. According to Fars News, the political positions of the Siniora government and the March 14 movement regarding the election of a new Lebanese president are "bound to the Saudi position."[26] Furthermore, Fars News argues that although the Saudis have stated that the "internationalization of the Lebanon crisis is not dangerous," in reality they only support the March 14 movement; they ignore the Lebanese opposition led by the Shi'a and Iranian-allied Hizballah.[27] Even the reformist newspaper *Hambastagi* considers Saudi policies in Lebanon to have taken an anti-Iranian turn since the September 11th

---

[23] RAND interview with Lebanese analyst, Beirut, February 2008.

[24] Nicholas Blanford, "Lebanon Warily Watches Its Salafis," *Christian Science Monitor*, 24 September 2008.

[25] RAND interview with Lebanese analyst, Beirut, February 2008.

[26] "Mavaze 14 Mars by mozoue Arabistan Saudi gereh khordeh [The Positions of March 14 Are Tied to the Saudi Position]," Fars News Agency, 29 April 2008.

[27] "Mavaze 14 Mars by mozoue Arabistan Saudi gereh khordeh [The positions of March 14 Are Tied to the Saudi Position]" (2008).

attacks on the United States and the Kingdom's increased cooperation with the United States.[28]

Saudi Arabia remains preoccupied with the specter of a Hizballah power and the subsequent empowerment of Iran's position in the Levant.[29] These concerns rose to the fore during the May 2008 controversy over Hizballah's communication and phone network, which was enabled by Iranian aid. The Lebanese government declared the system illegal, fearing that it would allow Hizballah to further erode the government's sovereignty and consolidate its position as a "micro-state."[30] The political conflict erupted into violence the same month, when Hizballah moved into the Sunni strongholds of west Beirut and sacked the principal media outlet owned by Saad Hariri.[31] To Saudi Arabia, the move illustrated the limits of coordination with Iran and showed how local dynamics can quickly undermine efforts at rapprochement.[32] Although Hizballah ceased its military action two days later, the incident confirmed its status as the country's undisputed political power.

Hizballah's "coup" and the political deadlock in Lebanon have opened a new chapter of confrontation between Saudi Arabia and Iran. Qatar, fearing the escalation of tensions between the two sides and seeking to both outmaneuver Saudi Arabia and accommodate Iran, quietly pushed for a diplomatic solution that was arrived at in Doha in late May. From Saudi Arabia's perspective, the Doha settlement only compounded the blow to its prestige dealt by Tehran—Riyadh's

---

[28] "Diplomasiye ashefte Arabistan dar Lobnan [Saudi Arabia's Messy Policy In Lebanon]," *Hambastagi Online*, 30 April 2008.

[29] This vision is also present in the West. See Pierre Rousselin, "Hezbollah's Coup d'Etat, *Le Figaro* (Paris), 9 May 2008.

[30] Nicholas Blanford, "Hezbollah Phone Network Spat Sparks Beirut Street War," *Christian Science Monitor*, 9 May 2008a; Hussein Shobokshi, "Lebanon: Before It Disappears," Al-Sharq Al-Awsat, 7 May 2008.

[31] Blanford (2008a); "Hizballah 'Seizes West Beirut,'" *al-Jazeera*, 9 May 2008.

[32] "Saudi Arabia Backs Extraordinary Arab League Meeting on Lebanon," *Arab News*, 9 May 2008; "Saudi Warns Lebanon Opposition Against Escalation," *Agence France Presse*, 8 May 2008.

"upstart" neighbor, tiny Qatar, had effectively bested it as the "go-to" mediator on Lebanon.[33]

Saudi Arabia Is Pursuing Multilateral Diplomacy to Counter Iranian Influence on the Palestinian Front

Whereas Saudi Arabia and Iran have engaged in a relatively nuanced balance between rivalry, coordination, and cooperation on the Lebanon issue, the Israeli-Palestinian question has brought a more confrontational tone to the forefront. As the political and security situation has evolved—with the 2006 Israel-Hizballah war and intra-Palestinian strife since 2006 resulting in the strengthening of Hizballah and Hamas, respectively—Iran has found itself in a stronger position regionally.

To counter Iran's support of Hamas, Saudi Arabia has been soliciting multilateral support from other Arab regimes, namely Egypt and Jordan, each of which regards Hamas as a threat to its own stability and Iran's rise as a danger to the region as a whole. In addition, through its 2002 peace initiative, Saudi Arabia has initiated an unofficial rapprochement with Israel, with whom it shares common concerns about Iran's nuclear ambitions. Noting this development, an Egyptian observer pointed to at least one positive development resulting from the rising threat from Iran: increased pragmatism in Arab diplomacy. "The old pan-Arab discourse of 'rejection' and 'confrontation' has shifted toward the vocabulary of 'engagement': engagement with Israel, engagement with old Arab rivals and, on occasion, engagement with Iran as a form of containment."[34]

Jordan shares a wide set of security concerns with Saudi Arabia regarding Iranian involvement in Gaza. Amman feels especially threatened by Hamas's empowerment, given the significance of the Palestinian population residing in Jordan and the residual memory of the 1970

---

[33] See David Sapsted, "Doha Commended on Lebanon Agreement," *The National*, 22 May 2008.

[34] RAND interview with Egyptian political science professor, Cairo, Egypt, February 2008.

Black September civil war. Underlying this concern is the more existential fear of becoming a battlefield for its neighbors—a sort of Middle Eastern Belgium.[35] "There is currently a form of triangular diplomacy by Israel, Saudi Arabia, and Egypt to prevent Jordan from becoming another Lebanon," noted one Jordanian analyst.[36] Among Jordanian officials, there is also the perception that Iran is seeking to increase its influence in Jordanian society through Shi'a proslytization among Sunnis, although evidence of this is anecdotal at best.[37] Officials in Amman did acknowledge that Iran had replaced al-Qaeda as Jordan's most pressing security threat. As a result, Jordan has been looking to renew its portfolio of alliances.[38] A Jordanian analyst pointed favorably to Jordan's burgeoning cooperation with Saudi Arabia, arguing that "Amman has provided the brains behind most Saudi initiatives, while Riyadh has the money."

Egypt finds its interests similarly aligned with Saudi Arabia's on the Palestine issue, with the escalation of conflict in Gaza a top concern. "Iran is now at Egypt's eastern doorstep," a former Egyptian official remarked.[39] Saudi-Egyptian cooperation is tempered, however, by Egyptian worries that Saudi assertiveness against Iran may undercut Cairo's traditional leadership on Arab issues. "Saudi activism is an annoying fact of life for Egypt," an Egyptian analyst noted, but with the caveat that "the saving grace for us is that Saudi 'initiatives' never amount to anything."

---

[35] See Curtis Ryan, *Jordan in Transition: From Hussein to Abdullah*, Boulder, Colo.: Lynne Rienner Press, 2002.

[36] RAND interview with Jordanian analyst, Amman, Jordan, March 2008.

[37] Daniel Byman, *Counterterrorism Trip Report: Israel and Jordan*, part of Toward a New U.S.-Middle East Strategy: A Saban Center at Brookings–Council on Foreign Relations Project, March 2008.

[38] Part of this renewed portfolio involves a rapprochement with Syria, which remains sustainable despite having been tested in the wake of the Hariri assassination and the subsequent Jordanian calls for Syrian withdrawal from Lebanon. See Curtis R. Ryan, "The Odd Couple: Ending the Jordanian-Syrian 'Cold War,'" *Middle East Journal*, Vol. 60, No. 1, Winter 2006.

[39] RAND interview with ex-foreign ministry official, Cairo, Egypt, February 2008.

Finally, Israel has also seen the value of a rapprochement with Levantine Arab countries in order to counter Iran's alliance with Hizballah and Syria. The peace that Israel established with Egypt in 1979 and Jordan in 1994 parallels the relationship that may be emerging between Israel and Saudi Arabia. In the aftermath of its war against Hizballah, Israel attempted to rally the Arab world against Iran, and Israeli officials publicly indicated that they considered Saudi Arabia a "moderate" state with whom cooperation was not only conceivable but desirable.[40] In addition, while expressing some qualms at the beginning, Israel did not oppose the 2007 arm sales deal between the United States and the GCC countries.[41]

Yet Israel's December 2008 incursion into Gaza and the resulting humanitarian crisis has undermined this warming of Israeli-Arab relations and, perhaps more favorably from Iran's perspective, exposed divisions in Riyadh's multilateral Arab approach. Saudi-Egyptian coordination on Gaza has faced concerted opposition from Qatar and Syria, who have attacked Cairo for failing to open the Rafah border crossing. Egypt, Saudi Arabia, and Jordan, in turn, have responded by boycotting a Syrian-backed Arab League summit in Doha. While some Arab commentators noted that these divisions had been at least partially bridged at the January 2009 Kuwait summit, there was opposition from Syria and Qatar to the revival of King Abdullah's 2002 peace initiative.[42] Iran, for its part, has reverted to its time-worn tradition of lambasting Arab regimes for their inaction and paralysis, while at the same time highlighting its own humanitarian contributions to Gaza.[43]

---

[40] Karby Leggett and Marcus W. Brauchli, "Israelis Reach Out to Arab Nations That Share Fear of Ascendant Iran," *The Wall Street Journal*, 2006, p. 1.

[41] See, for instance, Anthony Cordesman, "The Gulf Arms Sales: A Background Paper," Saudi-US Relations Information Service, 5 February 2008.

[42] "Surprise Reconciliation at Kuwait Summit," *The National* (UAE), 21 January 2009. For a dimmer view of the underlying Arab discord, see Marc Lynch, "Dueling Arab Summits," *Foreignpolicy.com*, 16 January 2009.

[43] For an example, see "Iran Slams Arab, International Inaction over Gaza," Fars News Agency, 4 January 2009.

What these dynamics reveal is that, like its efforts in the Gulf, Saudi Arabia's Levantine initiatives against Iran have been diluted by intra-Arab rivalries. This is particularly the case concerning the role of Syria, whose ties to Iran and rejectionist posture have been the source of frequent Saudi exasperation.

Saudi Arabia Has Focused on Isolating Syria to "Clip Iran's Wings"

Although once a principal recipient of Saudi aid, Syria has steadily run afoul of Riyadh since the ascension to power of Bashar al-Assad in 2000. Aside from the assassination of Rafik Hariri (a longtime Saudi ally) in February 2005, Syrian behavior after the summer 2006 Lebanon war helped further antagonize Riyadh. Bashar al-Assad's August 2006 speech deriding Arab leaders who failed to support Hizballah as "half men" reportedly left King Abdullah incensed, and a war of words soon followed.[44]

On both Lebanon and Palestine, Syria has emerged as the focal point of Saudi efforts against Iran. Saudi interlocutors noted that one of the Kingdom's top strategic goals in Lebanon was to "clip Iran's wings" by isolating Syria, primarily through the Hariri tribunal. Another Lebanese analyst pointed to Saudi Arabia's increasing ties with Turkey as a sort of circular diplomacy, designed to leverage Ankara's relations with Damascus to wean Syria away from Iran. As of early 2009, it appeared that Saudi Arabia had made some progress—even if largely symbolic—in isolating Syria's rejectionist posture on Gaza at the 2009 Arab summit in Kuwait, with Saudi newspapers proclaiming that Assad had arrived to the meeting weakened and that Syrian officials were "surprised" by the summit's spirit of reconciliation.[45]

Iranian news sources acknowledge the strain that Syria's support of Iranian policies has caused in Saudi-Syrian relations. A report

---

[44] Blanford (2007a).

[45] Saud Jarous, "Syria Surprised by Saudi Reconciliation—Sources" *al-Sharq al-Awsat* (English), 22 January 2009.

published by Iran's Arabic-language satellite TV channel al-Alam points out that the March 2008 Arab League conference in Damascus revealed increasing "disagreements among the Arab states."[46] According to the report, Saudi Arabia sent a low-level delegation to the conference because of its opposition to Syria's (and Iran's) policies in Lebanon. In addition, the Arab states, including Saudi Arabia, believe that Syria "facilitates Iranian policies" in the region and has allowed Iran to interfere in the Lebanon and Israeli-Palestinian issues.[47] They also objected to Syria inviting Iran to the Arab League meeting, viewing it as Iranian interference in Arab affairs. Responding tersely to Iran's offer to mediate between Syria and Saudi Arabia at the Damascus Summit, Saud al-Faysal stated that Saudi Arabia did not need Iran's help since it "has direct and strong relations with Syria."[48] From Iran's perspective, its offer to mediate between two Arab states does not appear provocative. After all, Iran believes that all three sides share a common enemy, Israel.

However, in practice, the sustainability of this potential three-way cooperation is grim. Indeed, Syria has been a useful ally for Iran so long as the relationship has not prevented Tehran from promoting its own goal in Lebanon, which is a militarily and politically strong Hizballah. In fact, rather than regard itself as a staunch ally of Syria, Iran seems to include Damascus in a balancing act that may evolve with time. If there is a possibility for Iran to settle with Saudi Arabia on the current power configuration in Lebanon and to make Hizballah's position a fait accompli, it seems feasible that Tehran and Hizballah may

---

[46] "Vagraye Arab dar conference Dameshgh [Arab Opinions at Damascus Conference]," *Al Alam News*, 2 April 2008.

[47] "Vagraye Arab dar conference Dameshgh" (2008).

[48] Entekhab News, "Vakonosh Saud al Faisal be pishnehad Iran baray e miyanjigari miyan e Dameshgh va Riyadh [Saudi al-Faisal's Reaction to Iran's Offer to Mediate Between Damascus and Riyadh]," 29 April 2008.

sacrifice Syria by accepting the creation of an international tribunal to Damascus's expense.[49]

Conclusion

In contrast to the Gulf, the Levant has witnessed more explicit rivalry and a Saudi effort to rollback Iran's influence. Yet even within the economic and political strategies pursued by each power on such issues as Lebanon and the Israeli-Palestinian question, there are nuanced "rules of the game" that tend to dampen sectarian strife. While the situation in Lebanon and the Israeli-Palestinian issue has led both powers to support rival groups in the region, Riyadh and Tehran have successfully managed their competition by finding grounds for cooperation when their mutual interests were at stake. However, Saudi Arabia must also deal with the fact that the Iranian regime as a whole is deeply and ideologically opposed to Israel and may not always act in a flexible and pragmatic fashion regarding the Levant.

The two potential vectors of change in the region are Hizballah and Syria. Hizballah's continued pressure on the Lebanese Siniora government and subsequent consolidation of its military and political power in the region have increased Iran's influence and made Saudi Arabia and other Arab states more willing to seek a balancing alliance that would involve Israel. Syria's emergence as a swing vote, given its ad hoc alliance with Iran on the Lebanese issue, could also provide some leverage to Saudi Arabia, but only if both Damascus and Riyadh are able to find a compromise on the Hariri issue—an unlikely scenario in the short run. What will be decisive in the Levant is Saudi Arabia and Iran's cost-benefit assessment of a cooperative relationship in the region. So far, the assessment has led both powers to pursue their rivalry through nonstate allies, but calculations may quickly change.

---

[49] David Schenker, *Saudi-Iranian Mediation on Hizballah: Will a Lebanon Deal Come at Syria's Expense*, Policy Watch 1204, Washington, D.C.: The Washington Institute for Near East Policy, February 2007; Slackman (2007a, 2007b).

CHAPTER FIVE

Conclusion: Key Findings and Implications for U.S. Policy

In the preceding chapters, we have explored the dynamics and evolution of Saudi-Iranian relations since 2003 across a number of different topical and geographic spheres. This study is intended to fill a gap in previous literature by using the bilateral relationship between these powers as a framework to assess important transformations in the Middle East security environment. Although not the sole drivers behind these shifts, the dynamics of confrontation, coordination, and engagement between Riyadh and Tehran have had important consequences for security, stability, and economic growth in the Gulf and the Levant. Previous post-2003 studies have often interpreted Saudi-Iranian relations using a dichotomous lens of either sectarian confrontation or pragmatic rapprochement. Yet the relationship as it is evolving today throughout the region appears to incorporate elements of both.

Much of this hybrid approach is not new; U.S. policymakers would do well to study the cyclical nature of the relationship, particularly during the pre-1979 era—in which Saudi Arabia and Iran had mutual security concerns and de facto shared leadership in the region—and during the mid-1990s warming of relations. These periods are illustrative for what they reveal about the capability of the two countries to reach an accommodation on regional order while minimizing deeper ideological and structural tensions. Similarly, they highlight some perennial "truths" about power relations in the Gulf that exist irrespective of U.S. policy preferences or the character of the regime in Tehran: Saudi Arabia has a deeply ingrained preference for an external balancer to Iran, while Iran will demand a more indigenous security system that would imply a de facto recognition of its primacy by Saudi Arabia.

Within this geometry of power, another enduring fact is that a weak Iraq will inevitably increase competition between Riyadh and Tehran as the two powers vie for influence.[1] Today, Riyadh is alarmed that the balance of power in Iraq is tilted squarely in favor of Iran and that Riyadh's traditional approach of soliciting an external balancer (the United States) has yielded little fruit.[2] With the release of the Iraq Study Group report in 2006, the 2007 NIE on Iran, and the announcement of an impending drawdown in Iraq, Saudi Arabia has detected a subtle shift in Washington's approach toward Iran that suggests a downgrading of the threat, a move toward strategic détente with Iran, and, most worrisome from Riyadh's point of view, a de facto acceptance of an Iranian-backed client regime in Baghdad.

Saudi Arabia has thus shifted from a posture of explicit confrontation toward Iran to a policy of guarded engagement in the Gulf that is believed to stand a better chance of moderating Iranian behavior. The broader GCC, despite its disunity and disarray, appears to be following suit. As noted by UK-based scholar Gerd Nonneman, a long-time analyst of Gulf politics:

> On the one hand they want a joint diplomatic strategy to avoid a nuclear-armed Iran but also they are saying we think we can engage Iran more effectively. We think we can take the sting out of this by engaging with Iran.[3]

---

[1]   This point was made by Chubin and Tripp (1996).

[2]   Henner Furtig has noted a fundamental shift in the regional balance of power from a triangular system—consisting of Iran, Iraq, and Saudi Arabia, with two of these powers balancing the third in different configurations since World War II—to a bilateral system where "Strangely enough, the external or at least non-Arab powers, i.e., the U.S. and Iran, are now the most powerful actors in the otherwise Arab Gulf region" (Furtig, 2007, p. 640).

[3]   Quoted in Lin Noueihed, "Analysis-Gulf Arabs Chart Delicate Course Between Iran, U.S.," Reuters, 10 January 2008. See also "Embracing Iran in Region May Affect Nuclear Plans," *Abha al-Watan*, translated by Open Source Center, GMP20071106614009, 6 November 2007.

The ultimate driver in this shift was confusion among the Gulf states over U.S. policy intentions: The 2006 Gulf Security Dialogue and the accompanying weapons sales, intended to shore up the confidence of the Gulf states, were effectively overtaken by the perception of a U.S.-Iranian coordination on Iraq and the need to secure a "seat at the table" before any U.S.-Iranian deal marginalizes the Arab states. Gulf states were further motivated by Iranian Supreme Leader Ali Khamenei's statement in January 2008, which implied that under the right circumstances, relations with the United States were possible.[4] Iran, for its part, has shown itself capable of tempering its criticism of Riyadh as a host to U.S. forces in the Gulf when it perceives greater economic and diplomatic benefits are to be gained.

Yet our research warns against viewing this cooperation in the Gulf as symptomatic of a comprehensive rapprochement. In the Gulf, Saudi Arabia is still attempting to balance and deter Iran through a conventional military buildup and cooperation with the larger GCC. Moreover, deep-seated structural and geostrategic differences are often reflected in other regional areas, even while tensions in the Gulf appear to be more muted or on the upswing. For example, just as the two states were taking tentative steps toward repairing relations in the wake of the 1991 Gulf war and the recognition of a shared threat from Saddam, there was jostling for influence among the newly independent states of the post-Soviet order, in the Caucasus and in Central Asia. Today, this oscillation between confrontation in one area and coordination in another is reflected in Riyadh's larger diplomatic approach toward Tehran—what one interlocutor described as "engagement in the Gulf, containment in Iraq and rollback in the Levant."[5]

As of late 2008, however, the balance sheet of this effort may suggest an impending course correction for Saudi Arabia. The Kingdom's "isolate and engage" policy has not improved the balance of power in its favor but rather just the opposite. Riyadh's Lebanese allies, the March 14 Alliance, were humiliated by Hizballah's brazen military incursion into West Beirut and the sacking of Saad Hariri's media out-

---

[4] For a good analysis of these shifts, see Partrick (2008).

[5] RAND interview with Saudi think-tank researcher, Jeddah, March 2007.

lets in May 2008. The Maliki government in Iraq has gained greater popular support inside Iraq and demonstrated its military prowess during mid-2008 counterinsurgency campaigns in Sadr City, Basrah, Amarah, and Diyala. Regional Arab consensus appears to be moving cautiously toward greater recognition of Maliki, with Riyadh appearing to be the odd man out. The Saudi-sponsored Mecca agreement was a diplomatic failure, and Iran's Palestinian ally, Hamas, has gained the upper hand over Fatah.

All of this suggests caution for U.S. policymakers who interpret the relationship as playing out uniformly and constantly across a number of subregions in the Middle East.

Toward a More Nuanced Understanding: This Study's Key Findings

Taking these historic and structural factors into account, the more specific findings of our study have important implications for U.S. policy:

Sectarianism Has Strained the Relationship, but It Is Not the Key Driver

Today, sectarian and ideological differences between the two states have had an "echo effect" on the region, but they are not the principal drivers in the policy calculus of each regime. Saudi Arabia may be over-estimating the effect of Iran's influence over Gulf Shi'a populations and may harbor more deep-seated fears about Iran's populist threat to the legitimacy and pan-Arab standing of the al-Saud. The royal family itself faces pressure from Salafi clerics (both inside and outside the formal religious bureaucracy) to take an anti-Shi'a position in its dealings with Iran. The ruling elite appear to have exploited or tacitly endorsed this rhetoric against Iran's ideological challenge, but the ultimate victims in this tactic have been Saudi Arabia's own Shi'a population.

Since mid-2007, the ruling family has taken some steps to curtail the issuance of more-strident *fatawa*—a sign of moderation that has received guarded recognition from Iran. For its part, Iran has tended to down play sectarianism in the bilateral relationship, criticizing anti-Shi'a rhetoric from Saudi Arabia, but often distinguishing between Saudi clerical voices and the regime itself.

In the Gulf, Tensions Are Moderated by Mutual Interest and GCC Diversity

Beginning in the 1990s, the two states have endeavored to manage the tenor of their relations in the Gulf, focusing on shared economic interests and bilateral security cooperation. Much of this stemmed from Tehran's effective abandonment of its policy of exporting the Revolution and attempting to incite Shi'a populations in Bahrain and Saudi Arabia. Riyadh's approach has also been tempered by the tendency of other Gulf states toward dialogue with Iran; Oman is a good case in point, as is Qatar's invitation to Ahmadinejad to attend the December 2007 GCC summit in Doha. GCC states are generally disunited in their views toward Iran—a disarray that implicitly favors Tehran and has forced Riyadh toward a more accommodating posture. For its part, Tehran's posture toward Saudi Arabia and the Gulf has been affected by an internal debate and conflicting voices; factions that emphasize the Gulf as a zone of economic enrichment and mutual cooperation frequently contend with those who take a more hegemonic view, preferring the instruments of threat and intimidation.

That said, there are several important flashpoints in the Gulf that bear watching; Riyadh is concerned that Shi'a unrest and activism in Saudi Arabia's Eastern Province, as well as in Bahrain and Kuwait, may give Iran new opportunities for influence. The ultimate drivers of this agitation, however, are rooted more in the political marginalization of these Shi'a communities, regime-sanctioned discrimination, and economic deprivation than any incitement from Iran. If these conditions are allowed to fester or deteriorate, local Shi'as will have greater incentives to look to Iran for patronage, which could exacerbate Saudi-Iran tensions.

Riyadh and Tehran Perceive Iraq as a Zero-Sum Game

Much focus has been directed at Iraq as an arena for "proxy" competition, particularly in the event of a U.S. withdrawal. Saudi Arabia's warnings that it will increase its intervention following a U.S. departure should be taken seriously, but its ability to support and influence Sunni factions should not be inflated. Thus, its role in containing Iran may be more limited than is realized.

A key theme is Saudi Arabia's desire to keep the United States involved as a balancer and, absent this, to play a role in shaping the outcome of any trilateral Iranian-U.S.-Iraqi talks. Sensing that this strategy may be eroding, Riyadh has recently taken steps to diversify and strengthen its contacts with a range of Iraqi political actors. Meanwhile, Iran has made overtures to Saudi Arabia about a sort of cooperative power-sharing relationship over Iraq that may mirror previous coordination on Lebanon, but that explicitly calls for the departure of U.S. forces. Riyadh likely sees this for what it is: an attempt to deprive Saudi Arabia of its external balancer and relegate it to the status of junior partner in the new regional order. Instead of true cooperation, the relationship over Iraq is likely to be defined as "managed rivalry," with a modicum of coordination and contact to prevent an escalation of sectarian conflict, which would benefit neither side.

Riyadh and Tehran Have Tried to Regulate Tensions over Iran's Nuclear Program

The advent of a nuclear-armed Iran would likely be perceived as an existential threat to Riyadh, possibly pushing Saudi Arabia to acquire its own countervailing deterrent. Current relations over the nuclear issue, however, are more muted than might be expected. In its approach, Riyadh appears to adhere more closely to the European line of treating the Iranian issue within the context of a WMD-free Middle East, which would include Israel. Such pronouncements are partly calculated to imply Riyadh's non-support for a U.S. strike, which Saudi Arabia perceives would engender both domestic public opposition and erode the al-Saud's legitimacy on the Arab stage. Iran, for its part, appears to see the nuclear issue as manageable. Through its official and unofficial press outlets, Iran has portrayed mutual harmony on the issue, often citing what it perceives to be Riyadh's acceptance of the program's peaceful nature.

Rivalry in the Levant Is More Explicit

If Saudi-Iranian relations in the Gulf and Iraq are based on engagement and containment, respectively, then the Levant is best characterized as an arena for more open competition and rivalry. Much of this stems from Saudi perception of the Iranian threat: In the normative realm of Saudi public perception and belief in the legitimacy of the monarchy, Iran's actions in the Arab-Israeli sphere do far more harm to the Saudis than its actions in Iraq. It was Hizballah's 2006 war with Israel that opened significant rifts between and among the Saudi clerical class and put the al-Saud in the awkward position of having been upstaged on the Israeli-Palestinian issue by a non-Arab, Shi'a power. Riyadh also likely perceives that to keep its influence in the pan-Arab realm it must take a more proactive stance on the Israeli-Palestinian issue, as well as Lebanon.

Much of the current effort involves Riyadh attempting to punish and isolate Syria through the Hariri tribunal, while tacitly and perhaps grudgingly supporting Turkish and Israeli efforts to bring Syria back into the Arab fold. In response, Iran has attempted to paint Saudi policies in the Levant as explicitly sectarian in nature in order to discredit its role as a broker, either on the Israeli-Palestinian issue or in Lebanon. The Iranian press has highlighted Riyadh's support to radical Salafi groups and has gone so far as to implicate it in the assassination of Hizballah commander Imad Mughniyah.

An important dimension of the relationship in the Levant is the way it conditions the views of local actors, particularly in Lebanon; outside meddling and interference can be used by competing Lebanese factions as justification for avoiding compromise.

Implications for U.S. Policy

Incorporating the themes outlined above, U.S. policy can better manage the implications of the Saudi-Iranian relationship in the following ways:

View Saudi Arabia Less as a Bulwark Against Iran and More as an Interlocutor

U.S.-Saudi interests are aligned against Iran in many ways, but Riyadh is unlikely to act in lockstep with Washington's strategy. Indeed, the current Saudi-centric containment strategy appears to have been over-taken by events, with Saudi Arabia pursuing a nuanced approach that incorporates elements of accommodation, engagement, and rollback. A U.S. paradigm that views Saudi Arabia solely through the lens of a confrontational proxy, with the expectation that Riyadh will employ all levers of influence at its disposal against Tehran, does not reflect regional reality or the pattern of interaction between Saudi Arabia and Iran. Riyadh has a demonstrated tendency to hedge its bets, to avoid taking stark policy decisions, and to keep multiple options open—especially in the context of what it perceives as inconsistent and ambiguous U.S. policies toward Iran. Moreover, regional observers see little role for Saudi Arabia as a real regional balancer against Iran, particularly in light of long-standing tensions within the GCC about Riyadh's dominance and activism.

In contrast to this balancing paradigm, voices in Saudi Arabia appear to see the Kingdom's role as a gateway for Iran to approach the United States. "We try to help Iran soften its language of international diplomacy toward the U.S.," noted one Saudi diplomat to RAND researchers in March 2007. "The Iranians come to us when they are rejected by the Chinese or Russians."[6] This view appears to be echoed by voices in Iran, albeit in ways that enhance Iran's leverage. In April 2007, Iran's conservative-dominated Majles (parliament) commissioned a study that argued that "improving relations with Saudi Arabia can increase Iranian diplomacy's negotiating power against West."[7]

The United States should seek to cultivate this Saudi mediating trend, encouraging Saudi outreach to Tehran while at the same time

---

[6]   RAND interview, March 2007.

[7]   "In the Most Recent Report by the Majlis Research Centre: Improving Relations with Saudi Arabia Can Increase Iranian Diplomacy's Negotiating Power Against West," *Aftab-e Yazd* (Tehran), translated by Open Source Center, IAP20070416011006, 16 April 2007.

working to resolve the regional arenas of competition between the two states, particularly on the Arab-Israeli front.

Seek Saudi Burden-Sharing in Iraq, but Not to Counteract Iran

As noted above, it is important that the United States not exaggerate Saudi Arabia's influence over Sunni factions in Iraq or view it as analogous to Iran's influence over Iraqi Shi'as. The Saudis themselves appear to recognize this and are diversifying the breadth and intensity of their contacts with a wide range of Iraqi political factions. The United States should encourage this trend, but with the explicit understanding that these levers should work toward the stabilization and equitable political development of Iraq, rather than the targeted rollback of Iranian influence. Already, Tehran is alarmed that the Sunni tribal strategy employed in al-Anbar against al-Qaeda could be replicated among southern Shi'a tribes against Iranian influence, and it likely views Saudi Arabia as a potential patron in this effort, despite the sectarian divide. Taken together with Tehran's long-standing perception of Riyadh's incitement of Sunni volunteers to Iraq, this could significantly exacerbate tensions, with destabilizing consequences for Iraq and the broader region.

The United States must acknowledge that the Iraqi people themselves will determine the extent and type of Iranian involvement in their affairs; soliciting an external counterweight to Iranian influence is unlikely to yield any positive results. One of the important indigenous buffers to Iranian interference is Iraqi nationalism, which could reassert itself following a U.S. withdrawal, even by a Shi'a-dominated government. Washington should expend great effort to allay Saudi fears about Iran's actual control over Iraqi Shi'as. To do this, the United States must carefully set the stage for the drawdown of U.S. forces—providing necessary security guarantees to Riyadh yet also communicating to the Iraqi government the importance of building institutions in a nonsectarian manner, particularly the Iraqi Security Forces, and integrating the Sunni-based Awakening Councils and Sons of Iraq into Iraqi political life. In light of these confidence-building measures, Saudi Arabia must be encouraged to expand its diplomatic contacts with Iraq, as with any neighboring country. Most specifically, Saudi

Arabia must be encouraged to open an embassy in Baghdad.[8] This would signal to Iran the necessity of acknowledging the country's links to the Sunni west, normalizing its relations with Iraq, and ending its policy of lethal aid to Shi'a militants.

Not only is the future Iraq at stake, but so are the larger suite of bilateral relations between Riyadh and Tehran. Indeed, a paper by an Iranian think tank argued that cooperation between Saudi Arabia and Iran concerning Iraq can be a "gateway" to a broader understanding on such issues such as Iran's nuclear technology, OPEC, and security in the Gulf.[9]

Encourage Saudi Initiatives on the Arab-Israeli Front

As this study has shown, Iran's more enduring challenge to Saudi Arabia is not necessarily as a conventional military power but rather as a state that constantly seeks to play a spoiler role in Arab-Israeli affairs. Iran's Levantine nonstate allies, Hizballah and Hamas, are players in this strategy, dependent on Syria as a key conduit. Much of the focus by Arab states (and Israel and Turkey) is geared toward eliminating this conduit by wrestling Syria away from Tehran. Yet Riyadh is unlikely to find a compromise with Damascus on the Hariri issue, and given the durability and robustness of the Tehran-Damascus axis, energy might be better expended on other areas. Specifically, regional peace initiatives such as that put forward by Saudi King Abdullah are proactive efforts that help isolate Iranian rejectionism on the Arab-Israeli front, even if they ultimately fall short of achieving a lasting peace. Washington should be cognizant, however, of how intra-Arab rivalries can undermine Saudi initiatives on the Palestinian issue and against Iran.

Push for Domestic Reform in Saudi Arabia and the Gulf to Mitigate Sectarianism

The sectarian dimension of Saudi-Iran relations stems from political inequity among the Gulf Shi'as and fears by Riyadh and other Sunni

---

[8]   As of June 2008, Kuwait, the UAE, and Bahrain had all announced their intentions to open embassies in Baghdad.

[9]   Hadyan (2006).

regimes that these populations are susceptible to Iranian influence. The mid-1990s have shown that genuine efforts toward integration and dialogue between Gulf rulers and their Shi'a populations has the effect of lessening Iran's attractiveness as an external patron. Conversely, the hardening of anti-Shi'a discrimination and backtracking on reforms could make Shi'a public opinion swing more toward more radical domestic factions who are influenced by Iran or who seek to emulate the Hizballah model in the Gulf. More equitable power sharing, in which hard-line Salafi clerics are denied a prominent platform to voice their anti-Shi'a views, will also improve Saudi-Iranian bilateral relations and reduce sectarian tensions. Ultimately, the United States and regional governments must acknowledge that the threat of an Iranian-backed Shi'a fifth column in the Gulf is overblown, but that stagnation on reform toward the Shi'as could make these fears a self-fulfilling prophecy. Washington should avoid viewing sectarian tension as an inevitable feature of the bilateral relationship, but rather a by-product of fundamental power inequities in the Gulf that can be mitigated through reform. At the same time, Washington should understand that the scope and pace of any reforms will be determined by the Gulf states themselves.

Avoid Actions That Inflame Iranian Perceptions of External Meddling in Its Affairs

Iran has great reason to fear external meddling in its internal affairs, given the 1953 Mossadegh coup. The fall of Saddam has only heightened this perception, and Tehran fears that a decentralized Iraq could increase dissent among the ethnic and sectarian groups within its own borders. The Sunni Baluch in Iran's Sistan-va Baluchestan province, the Kurds in Kordestan, and ethnic Arabs in Khuzestan are potential concerns. At times, Iran has perceived the hand of Saudi Arabia behind this agitation, particularly in Baluchestan and in light of the purported growth of Salafi ideology there. While much of this fear is undoubtedly exaggerated, Washington can mitigate it as a source of Saudi-Iranian tension by abandoning the idea that domestic dissent inside Iran can be engineered from the outside. If, on the other hand, this idea grows, there is the potential for what one Saudi interlocutor called a "dirty war" escalating among non-state groups backed by each country, to the detriment of U.S. interests and regional stability.

Pursue Saudi-Iranian Endorsement of Multilateral Security for the Gulf

This study has shown that the Gulf is one arena where bilateral tensions have been regulated by a host of shared interests. Capitalizing on this dynamic, the United States should work toward a more cooperative Gulf security arrangement that includes the United States but that also recognizes Iran as a valid player. U.S. involvement would be crucial to help assuage Saudi and Gulf concerns about Iranian dominance.

A conflict-regulating "concert" system for the Gulf, like the OSCE, bears further consideration in this regard. In this sort of forum, mutual threat perceptions are aired and conflict-reduction measures are pursued. Cooperation in the maritime area would be a useful area of focus for such a forum (such as work on a regional incidents-at-sea agreement), particularly given the potential for miscalculation and escalation in critical waterways, such as the Strait of Hormuz.[10]

This proposed structure is not without its drawbacks: The Saudi preference for an external, nonregional security guarantor has been noted, and Iran continues to view such U.S.-sponsored proposals as a code for increased U.S. hegemony. Smaller Gulf states are unlikely to join until the future of Iraq is secured, and many will continue their preference for bilateral ties with the United States, fearful of Saudi Ara-

---

[10] For proposals, background, and criticism of this approach, see Andrew Rathmell, Theodore W. Karasik, and David C. Gompert, *A New Persian Gulf Security System*, Santa Monica, Calif.: RAND Corporation, IP-248-CMEPP, 2003; Michael Kraig, "Assessing Alternative Security Frameworks for the Persian Gulf," *Middle East Policy*, Vol. 11, No. 3, fall 2004; Joseph A. Kechichian, *Security Efforts in the Arab World: A Brief Examination of Four Regional Organizations*, Santa Monica, Calif.: RAND Corporation, N-3570-USDP, 1994; Christian-Peter Hanelt and Almut Möller, *Security Situation in the Gulf Region Involving Iran, Iraq and Saudi Arabia as Regional Powers: Policy Recommendations for the European Union and the International Community*, Discussion Paper for Europe and the Middle East, Bertelsmann Stiftung and Center for Applied Policy Research, July 2007; Richard Russell, "The Collective Security Mirage," *Middle East Policy*, Vol. 12, No. 4, 2005b; Kenneth Pollack, "Securing the Gulf," *Foreign Affairs*, Vol. 83, No. 4, 2003, and James A. Russell, "Whither Regional Security in a World Turned Upside Down?" *Middle East Policy*, Vol. 14, No. 2, Summer 2007.

bia's dominance.[11] In addition, the GCC's internal political tensions, such as Shi'a marginalization, make the implementation of this structure more problematic. As we have seen, much of the Gulf regimes' threat perception of Iran is a mirror of their own domestic insecurity.[12] Thus, internal reform and liberalization remain key priorities.

Despite these obstacles, the best approach is to work toward a new paradigm that does not focus on a specific threat, but rather provides an open-ended security forum where regional states can discuss and address a range of regional challenge. Such an approach ultimately stands a better chance than a more traditional balancing paradigm that imparts too much confidence in Riyadh's will and capabilities to act as a viable counterweight to Iran.

---

[11] This point was made repeatedly in the Gulf to RAND during interviews from February 2006 to March 2007.

[12] This issue was raised by Matteo Legrenzi, "Mutual Threat Perceptions in the Gulf," *Middle East Policy*, Vol. 14, No. 2, 2007, pp. 117–118

Bibliography

Abd al-Latif, Omayma, "The Shia-Sunni Divide: Myths and Reality," *al-Ahram Weekly*, 1–7 March 2007.

Abdul-Hussain, Hussain, "Standing up to Killers: Syria Must Answer for Its Murders in Lebanon," *The Washington Post*, June 14, 2007.

Abed, Karim, "Khalfiyat wa Ahdaf al-Tadakhul al-Irani fi al-Iraq [The Background of and the Goals behind the Iranian Interference in Iraq]," *al-Hayat*, 20 May 2007.

AbuKhalil, As'ad, "Determinants and Characteristics of the Saudi role in Lebanon: The Post-Civil War Years," in Madawi al-Rasheed, ed., *Kingdom Without Borders: Saudi Arabia's Political, Religious and Media Frontiers*, London: Hurst and Company, 2008, pp. 79–97.

Abu Nasr, Donna, "Saudi Arabia Treads Carefully as It Tries to Douse Threat of Sectarianism," Associated Press, 2 February 2007.

————, "Saudi Clerics Criticize Shiites for Destabilizing," Associated Press, 1 June 2008.

Adler, Alexandre, "Les mystères de la mort d'Imad Mughnieh, [Mysteries Around the Death of Imad Mughniyeh]," *Les Matins de France Culture*, 15 February 2008. As of 17 December 2008:
http://www.radiofrance.fr/chaines/france-culture2/emissions/matins/fiche.php?diffusion_id=59905

"Adm bazgashti sefarat Arabistan dar Aragh be masael amniyati bar migardad [The Return of the Saudi Embassy to Iraq Will Be Determined by Security Conditions]," Mehr News Agency, 28 April 2008. As of 17 December 2008:
http://www.mehrnews.com/fa/NewsPrint.aspx?NewsID=670999

Afrasiabi, Kaveh, "Saudi-Iran Tension Fuels Wider Conflict," *Asia Times*, 6 December 2006. As of 17 December 2008:
http://www.atimes.com/atimes/Middle_East/HL06Ak04.html

"Ahmadinejad Calls Zionist Regime a 'Stinking Corpse,'" Islamic Republic News Agency, Tehran, 8 May 2008.

al-Anani, Khalil, "Limadha La Tahdur Iran al-Qimma al-Arabiya Kamuraqib? [Why Not Invite Iran to Attend the Arab League as a Spectator?]," *al-Hayat* Newspaper, 21 March 2007.

"Al-Arrab Contracting Company," *Middle East Economic Digest*, Vol. 52, No. 9, 26 February–6 March, 2008.

Al-Arabiya, "Banorama: Kayf Yanthur al-Arab Iran? [Panorama: How Do Arabs View Iran?]," February 26, 2007.

"Al-Asad Comments on Israeli Raid, Iranian Nuclear Issue, Other Issues," *al-Watan* (Doha), translated by Open Source Center, GMP20080427637004, 27 April 2008.

al-Dakhil, Khalid, "al-Taakul al-Dawr al-Misri fi al-Mintaqa [The Erosion of the Egyptian Role in the Region]," al-Arabiyya.net, 5 July 2006. As of 18 December 2008:
http://www.alarabiya.net/views/2006/07/05/25397.html

al-Dhaydi, Mshari, "Uhadhir an Taqdhi Alihi al-Ama'im [I Warn the Religious Establishment]," *al-Sharq al-Awsat*, 19 July 2007.

al-Durusi, Salman, "Al-Shaykh Khalifah bin Salman: Al-Khalij La Yatahammal Harb Jadidah [Sheikh Khalifah Bin Salman: The Gulf Cannot Take Another War]," *Al-Sharq Al-Awsat*, 28 July 2007.

al-Fahd, Nasr, "Letter on the Legitimacy of Swearing at the Shi'a," n.d. As of 12 April 2006:
http://www.tawhed.ws

———, "Response to the Rafida on Their Indictment of the Companions," n.d. As of 12 April 2006:
http://www.tawhed.ws

Algar, Hamid, *Wahhabism: A Critical Essay,* North Haledon, N.J.: Islamic Publications International, 2002.

al-Gharib, Muhammad Abdallah, *"Wa Ja'a Dur al-Majus [And Then Came the Turn of the Magi]*, n.p., 1983., As of 17 December 2008:
http://www.tawhed.ws/a?i=402

al-Hakeem, Mariam, "Saudi Arabia Refutes Iranian Allegation about Murder of Hezbollah Commander," *Gulf News*, 21 April 2008.

al-Hasan, Bilal, "Ahmadinejad's Grave Mistake: The Theory of Vacuum Filling," *al-Sharq al-Awsat* (in Arabic), 2 September 2007.

al-Humayd, Tariq, "al-Insihab al-Amriki al-Sakut al-Thani [The American Withdrawal: The Second Defeat]," *al-Sharq al-Awsat*, 9 October 2007a.

———, "Ala Matha Tufawad Washington Tehran? [What Will Washington Negotiate with Tehran?]," *al-Sharq al-Awsat*, 15 October 2007b.

al-Husseini, Huda, "Syria Attacks Saudi Arabia to Reaffirm Its Control of Lebanon," *al-Sharq al-Awsat*, 24 August 2007.

————, "Middle East: No Solutions Before Bush Leaves," *Al-Sharq Al-Awsat*, 23 April 2008.

al-Jazeera, "al-Kharita al-Madhhabiya fi al-Sa'udiya [The Map of Sects in Saudi Arabia]," 6 June 2003. As of 18 December 2008:
http://www.aljazeera.net/NR/exeres/C65C2C02-0CF9-4B10-8CD3-5B63F1EDBF51.htm

al-Khazin, Jihad, "Al-Maradh al-Arabi [The Arab Disease]," Saudi in Focus Web site, 6 April 2007. As of 18 June 2008:
http://www.saudiinfocus.com/ar/show_art_det.asp?artid=320

al-Khudayr, Ali bin Khudayr, "Fatwa on the Shi'a," Web page, Arabic, n.d. As of 17 December 2008:
http://www.tawhed.ws

"Al-Manar Reports on Saudi-Iranian Talks, Initial Understanding on Lebanese File," *al-Manar Television* (Beirut), translated by Open Source Center, GMP20070126644001, 26 January 2007.

al-Mani, Saleh, "The Ideological Dimension in Saudi-Iranian Relations," in Jamal S. al-Suwaidi, *Iran and the Gulf: A Search for Stability,* Abu Dhabi, Emirates Center for Strategic Studies and Research, 1996.

al-Marhun, Abdul Jalil Zaid, "al-'Amn al-Khalij b'ad Harb al-'Iraq [Gulf Security After the Iraq War]," Riyadh, Saudi Arabia: Institute for Diplomatic Studies, 2005.

al-Munim Sa'id, 'Abd, "al-Kharuj al-Amriki min al-'Iraq! [The American Withdrawal from Iraq]," *al-Sharq al-Awsat*, 18 January 2008.

al-Nabi al-Ukri, 'Abd, "Mutatallabat wa Tab'iat al-Islah al-Khaliji [Requirements and Development of Reform in the Gulf]," unpublished, undated paper provided to the authors, Manama, Bahrain, November 2006.

al-Qassemi, Sultan, "Gulf States May Continue to Ignore Iraq at Their Own Peril," *The National* (U.A.E.) June 21, 2008.

al-Rasheed, Madawi, *A History of Saudi Arabia,* New York: Cambridge University Press, 2007a.

————, *Contesting the Saudi State: Islamic Voices from a New Generation,* New York: Cambridge University Press, 2007b.

al-Rashid, Abd al-Rahman, "Lihathihi al-Asbab Naksha Iran [For These Reasons We Fear Iran]," *Al-Sharq Al-Awsat*, 18 April 2006.

————, "Khiyar Iraq: Namuthij Iran um al-Khalij [Iraq's Choice: The Model of Iran or the Gulf]," *al-Sharq al-Awsat*, 19 February 2009

al-Saffar, Shaykh Hassan, *Al-Madhhab wa al-Watan [Sect and Homeland]*, Beirut: Arab Foundation for Studies and Publishing, 2006.

———, "La wa Lan Nuqbil Aya' Marja'n Takfiri'an wa Arfad Tadkhal aya' Marja' fi al-Shu'un al-Siyasi al-Dakhili li-Biladna, [We Do Not and I Will Not Welcome Any *Marja'* (Spiritual Reference) That Promotes *Takfir* (Excommunication) and We Oppose the Interference of Any *Marja'* in the Internal Political Affairs of Our Country]," *al-Risala*, 16 February 2007.

al-Said, Radwan, "Qimat al-Inqisam al-Arabi ... Hal Tan'aqid? [The Summit of Divisions . . . Will It Convene?] *al-Sharq al-Awsat*, 16 January 2009.

al-Sarhan, Sa'ud Salah, "Nahwa Marja'iyya Shi'a Mustaqlila fi al-Khalij [Toward an Independent Shi'a Source of Emulation]," *al-Sharq al-Awsat*, 24 February 2003.

al-Sayf, Shaykh Tawfiq, *Nathiriyat al-Sulta fi al-Fiqh al-Shi'i* [Theories of Political Power in Shiite Jurisprudence], Beirut: Center for Arabic Culture, 2002.

al-Shayji, Abdullah K., "Mutual Realities, Perceptions and Impediments Between the GCC States and Iran," in Lawrence Potter and Gary G. Sick, eds., *Security in the Persian Gulf: Origins, Obstacles and the Search for Consensus*, New York: PalgraveMacmillan, 2002.

"Al-Sira' al-Ta'ifi fi al-Iraq wa al-Mintaqah [The Sectarian Conflict in Iraq and the Region)," al-Jazeera Television Network, Bila Hudud [Without Boarders] Program, aired 20 January 2007. As of 17 December 2008:
http://www.aljazeera.net/channel/archive/archive?ArchiveId=1038690

al-Tamimi, Jumana, "Rivals Turn Up Heat on Siniora," *Gulf News*, 9 January 2007.

al-Umar, Nasr, homepage, no date. As of 18 December 2008:
http://www.almoslim.net/

al-Zarqawi, Abu Musab, "Hal Ataka Hadith al-Rawafidh? [Has Word of the Rejectionists (Shiites) Reached You?]," audio recording, no date. As of 15 October 2007:
http://www.tawhed.ws/r?i=4048

"Analysis: Arab Dilemma Over Iran's Nuclear Program," BBC Monitoring, translated by Open Source Center, FEA20070627206546, 27 June 2007.

"Analysis of GCC Countries' Stances Toward Possible US-Iran War," *al-Sharq al-Awsat* (London), translated by Open Source Center, GMP20070923913004, 23 September 2007 [Article by Abd-al-Rahman al-Rashid (Part 1 of 2): "Will the Gulf Countries Remain Neutral in the War?"].

"Analysis: Survey of Iran's Arabic Satellite TV *al-Alam*," *Iran: Open Source Center Analysis*, GMF20070703684001, 3 July 2007.

Athanasiadis, Iason, "Sectarian Battles Spill Beyond Iraq; Sunnis, Shiites Eye Spoils for a Cold War Victory," *Washington Times*, 13 December 2006.

"Ayat Azam Makaram, Nouri va Safi dar mahkoumiyat e fatway e muftihaye Saudi [Grand Ayatollahs Makaram, Nouri, and Safi Condemn Fatwas Issued by Saudi Clerics]," *Iranian Student News Agency,* 23 July 2007.

Badib, Sa'ad, *Al-Alaqat al-Sau'audia al-Iraniya 1932–1983 [Saudi-Iranian Relations 1932–1983],* London: The Center for Iranian-Arab Relations, 1994.

Bahgat, Gawdat, "Iranian-Saudi Rapprochement. Prospects and Implications," *World Affairs,* Vol. 162, No. 3, Winter 2000.

———, "Nuclear Proliferation: The Case of Saudi Arabia," *Middle East Journal,* Vol. 60, No. 3, Summer 2006.

"Bahrainis Protest Against Iran Province Claim," *Reuters,* 14 July 2007.

Baker, James A. III, and Lee H. Hamilton, co-chairs, with Lawrence S. Eagleburger, Vernon E. Jordan, Jr., Edwin Meese III, Sandra Day O'Connor, Leon E. Panetta, William J. Perry, Charles S. Robb, Alan K. Simpson, *The Iraq Study Group Report: The Way Forward—A New Approach,* authorized ed., New York: Vintage Books, 2006.

Baker, Peter, and Robin Wright, "Iraq, Jordan See Threat to Election from Iran; Leaders Warn Against Forming Religious State," *The Washington Post,* 8 December 2004, p. A01.

Barnett, Michael N., and F. Gregory Gause, III, "Caravans in Opposite Directions: Society, State, and the Development of Community in the Gulf Cooperation Council," in Emanuel Adler and Michael N. Barnett, eds., *Security Communities,* Cambridge Studies in International Relations, Cambridge, England: Cambridge University Press, 1998.

Barzegar, K., "Vaghaye-e 11 september: roshd-e radicalism sonni va challeshha-e jaded-e amniyati dar hoze-e Khalije Fars [Consequences of 9/11: Expansion of Sunni Radicalism and Security Challenges in the Persian Gulf]," Center for Strategic Research, Foreign Policy Research Division, Expediency Council, 2002. As of 17 December 2008:
http://www.csr.ir/departments.aspx?abtid=07&&semid=330

BBC Monitoring, "Iran Paper Says Saudi Agents Wage 'Psychological Warfare' Against Iranian Pilgrims," Mardom-Salari Web site, July 11, 2007.

———, "Saudi Arabia Fingerprints Iranian Student Pilgrims," Fars News Agency, July 11, 2008.

BBC Monitoring Middle East, "Iran Women Pilgrims Visit Baqi Cemetery in Medina for First Time—Agency," 9 June 2008.

Beehner, Lionel, "Iran's Saudi Counterweight," Council on Foreign Relations, 16 March 2007. As of 17 December 2008:
http://www.cfr.org/publication/12856/irans_saudi_counterweight.html?breadcru mb=%2Fregion%2F413%2Fsaudi_arabia

bin Salman, Faisal, *Iran, Saudi Arabia, and the Gulf: Power Politics in Transition,* London: I. B. Tauris, 2003.

Blanford, Nicholas, "Is Iran Driving New Saudi Diplomacy?" *Christian Science Monitor,* 16 January 2007a.

———, "Chaos Returns to Troubled Lebanon," *Jane's Defence Weekly,* Vol. 44, No. 22, 30 May 2007b.

———, "Hezbollah Phone Network Spat Sparks Beirut Street War," *Christian Science Monitor,* 9 May 2008a.

———, "Lebanon Warily Watches its Salafis," *The Christian Science Monitor,* 24 September 2008b.

Boettcher, Mike, and Ingrid Arnesen, "South America's 'Tri-Border' Back on Terrorism Radar," *CNN,* 8 November 2002.

"Boosting Philippine-Iran Ties," *Manila Times,* 19 April 2008.

Bradley, John R., "Iran's Ethnic Tinderbox," *Washington Quarterly,* Vol. 30, No. 1, Winter 2006–2007.

Byman, Daniel, *Counterterrorism Trip Report: Israel and Jordan,* part of Toward a New U.S.-Middle East Strategy: A Saban Center at Brookings–Council on Foreign Relations Project, March 2008. As of 17 December 2008: http://www.cfr.org/publication/16183/counterterrorism_trip_report.html?breadcru mb=%2Fthinktank%2Ftanusmes%2Freports

Byman, Daniel L. and Kenneth Pollack, *Things Fall Apart: Containing the Spillover from an Iraqi Civil War,* Brookings Institution, Saban Center for Middle East Policy, January 2007.

"Cairo Political Analysts View Implications of Iranian-Saudi Rapprochement," *al-Misri al-Yawm* (Cairo), translated by Open Source Center, GMP20070309007003, 9 March 2007.

Center for Strategic Research, "Nazm-e Jadid-e Mantaghei dar khalije fars dar parto-e taamolate jomhuriye eslamiye Iran va Arabestan-e Saudi [New Regional Order in the Persian Gulf Under Iran and Saudi Arabia Cooperation]," Foreign Policy Research Division, Expediency Council, 2006. As of 17 December 2008: http://www.csr.ir/departments.aspx?abtid=04&&semid=63

Chubin, Shahram, *Iran's Nuclear Ambitions,* Washington, D.C.: Carnegie, 2006.

Chubin, Shahram, and Charles Tripp, "Iran-Saudi Arabia: Relations and Regional Order," *Adelphi Paper,* Vol. 204, London: International Institute for Strategic Studies, Oxford University Press, 1996.

Cole, Juan, "A Shi'a Crescent? The Regional Impact of the Iraq War," *Current History,* Vol. 105, No. 687, January 2006.

"Commander Warns Against Spread of Wahhabism in East Iran," Iranian Student News Agency, translated by Open Source Center, IAP20080308950072, 8 March 2008.

"Commentary Details Iran-Saudi Religious, Political Clash in Iraq," Persian Press, *Rahbord* (Tehran), IAP20061113336001, 16 May 2006 [Commentary by Hamid Hadyan: "Exploring Iran-Saudi Arabia Relations in Light of New Regional Conditions"].

Cordesman, Anthony, "The Gulf Arms Sales: A Background Paper," Saudi-US Relations Information Service, 5 February 2008.

———, "Security Challenges and Threats in the Gulf: A Net Assessment," Saudi-US Relations Information Service, 25 March 2008. As of 17 December 2008: http://www.saudi-us-relations.org/articles/2008/ioi/080325-cordesman-challenges.html

Crane, Keith, Rollie Lal, and Jeffrey Martini, Iran's Political, Demographic, and Economic Vulnerabilities, Santa Monica, Calif.: RAND Corporation, MG-693-AF, 2008. As of 10 February 2009: http://www.rand.org/pubs/monographs/MG693/

Crystal, Jill, "Political Reform and the Prospects for Democratic Transition in the Gulf," *Fundación para leas Relaciones Internacionales ye el Diálogo Exterior (FRIDE)*, Working Paper, 11 July 2005.

Dakiki, Paul, "Iran-Saudi Arabia Confrontation Play Out in Hamas-Fatah Talks," *Asia News*, 8 February 2007.

Dargin, Justin, "Qatar's Natural Gas: The Foreign Policy Driver," *Middle East Policy*, Vol. 14, No. 3, fall 2007, pp. 136–147.

Dawlat al-Ahsa wa al-Qatif, homepage, no date. As of 18 December 2008: http://www.alahssa-alkateef.com

"Diplomasiye ashefte Arabistan dar Lobnan [Saudi Arabia's Messy Policy In Lebanon]," *Hambastagi Online*, 30 April 2008. As of 17 December 2008: http://www.hamshahrionline.ir/News/?id=52889

Ebrahimi-far, Tahereh, "Olguhaye etemad sazi dar mantagheye Khalij-e Fars [The Patterns of Confidence Building Measures in the Persian Gulf]," Iranian Ministry of Foreign Affairs, Office of Political and International Studies, Tehran, 2001.

Ehteshami, Anoushiravan, "Iran's International Posture After the Fall of Baghdad," *Middle East Journal,* Vol. 58, No. 2, Spring 2004.

"Embracing Iran in Region May Affect Nuclear Plans," *Abha al-Watan*, translated by Open Source Center, GMP20071106614009, 6 November 2007.

"Emirates Will Start Pumping Gas from Qatar Despite Saudi Objections," Associated Press, 27 June 2007.

England, Andrew, "Arab Street Warms to Showman Ahmadi-Nejad," *Financial Times*, 6 April 2007.

Entekhab News, "Tavafogh sazmanhaye etelaati keshvarhay e mantaghe jahat brandazi dolat Aragh khbar dad [Agreement Among Regional Countries' Intelligence Agencies to Overthrow Maliki Government]," 12 July 2007a. As of 17 December 2008: http://www.tiknews.net/print/?ID=44132

———, "Tasbiyat ghodrat e Iran ba didar Ahmadinejad is Mecca [Ahamdinejad's Visit to Mecca Strengthens Iran's Power]," 28 December 2007b.

———, "Vaknesh Hosseini beh bayaniyeh Arabestan va France [Hosseini's Reaction to French and Saudi Statements]," 17 January 2008.

———, "Vakonosh Saud al Faisal be pishnehad Iran baray e miyanjigari miyan e Dameshgh va Riyadh [Saudi al-Faisal's Reaction to Iran's Offer to Mediate Between Damascus and Riyadh]," 29 April 2008.

"'Experts' Warn US Plan Uses Arab States to Cause Sunni Shia Split," Persian Press, Hezbollah (Tehran), translated by Open Source Center, IAP20070119011004, 14 January 2007.

"Ezam heyethay e namayandegi Arab beh Aragh, baraye rouyarouyi ba Iran nist [The Dispatch of Arab Diplomats to Iraq Is Not Meant to Confront Iran]," Fars News Agency, 28 April 2008. As of 17 December 2008: http://www.farsnews.com/printable.php?nn=870209493

Fahs, Hasan, "Abd al-Hadi LilHayat: Ay Sidam Irani-Amriki Sayas'ub Dhabtuhu Li'an Sahatuhu Wasi'ah wa al-Imkanat Kabira [Abd al-Hadi to al-Hayat Newspaper: Any American-Iranian Confrontation Would Be Difficult to Contain Because the Front Is Wide and the Resources Are Huge]," *al-Hayat*, 9 February 2007. As of 17 December 2008: http://www.daralhayat.com/special/dialogues/02-2007/Item-20070208-a290274e-c0a8-10ed-008d-41f2af2c1c24/story.html

Fandy, Mamoun, "al-'Iraq: Ja'izat al-'Arab al-Kubra, [Iraq: The Great Arab Prize]," *al-Sharq al-Awsat*, 9 June 2008.

"Fatah al-Islam," *Jane's World Insurgency and Terrorism*, 26 June 2007.

Fathi, Nazila, "Wipe Israel 'Off the Map' Iranian Says," *International Herald Tribune*, 27 October 2005.

Fattah, Hala, "'Wahhabi' Influences, Salafi Responses: Shaikh Mahmud Shukri and the Iraqi Salafi Movement, 1745–1930," *Journal of Islamic Studies,* Vol. 14, No. 2, 2003.

Fattah, Hassan M., "Bickering Saudis Struggle for an Answer to Iran's Rising Influence in the Middle East," *The New York Times*, 22 December 2006.

———, "U.S. Iraq Role is Called Illegitimate by Saudi King," *The New York Times*, 29 March 2007.

"First Round of Al-Zawahiri's Open Interview Released," translated by Open Source Center, FEA20080402611748, 2 April 2008.

Free State of Asir, homepage, no date. As of 18 December 008: http://www.aseer.com

Furtig, Henner, *Iran's Rivalry with Saudi Arabia Between the Gulf Wars,* New York: Ithaca Press, 2006.

———, "Conflict and Cooperation in the Persian Gulf: The Interregional Order and US Policy," *Middle East Journal*, Vol. 61, No. 4, fall 2007.

Garvey, John, *Protracted Contest: Sino-Indian Rivalry in the Twentieth Century,* Seattle, Wa.: University of Washington Press, 2002.

Gasiorowski, Mark, "The New Aggressiveness in Iran's Foreign Policy," *Middle East Policy*, Vol 14, No. 2, Summer 2007.

Gause, F. Gregory, III, "Saudi Arabia: Iraq, Iran and the Regional Power Balance and the Sectarian Question," *Strategic Insights,* February 2007a.

———, "Threats and Threat Perceptions in the Persian Gulf Region," *Middle East Policy*, Vol. 14, No. 2, Summer 2007b.

Ghadry, Farid, "Tit for Hariri Tat for Mughniyeh?," *Reform Party of Syria,* 10 April 2008.

Girard, Renaud, "The Calculated Provocations of the Islamist Iranian President," *Le Figaro* (Paris), 19 December 2005.

Guitta, Olivier, "First Target for Iran: Qatar?" *Middle East Times*, 26 November 2007.

Hadyan, Hamid, "Exploring Iran-Saudi Relations in Light of New Regional Conditions," *Rahbord* (Tehran), translated by Open Source Center, IAP20061113336001, 16 May 2006.

Halliday, Fred, *Nation and Religion in the Middle East,* Boulder, Colo.: Lynne Rienner Publishers, 2000.

Hanelt, Christian-Peter, and Almut Möller, *Security Situation in the Gulf Region Involving Iran, Iraq and Saudi Arabia as Regional Powers: Policy Recommendations for the European Union and the International Community,* Discussion Paper for Europe and the Middle East, Bertelsmann Stiftung and Center for Applied Policy Research, July 2007. As of 17 December 2008: http://www.cap.lmu.de/download/2007/2007_Gulf_Security.pdf

Hanizadeh, Hassan, "Iran, Saudi Arabia Open a New Chapter in Regional Cooperation," *Tehran Times*, 14 June 2008.

Haykel, Bernard, "Saudis United," blog post, Middle East Strategy at Harvard, 16 December 2007. As of 18 December 2008:
http://blogs.law.harvard.edu/mesh/2007/12/saudis_united/

Hegghamer, Thomas, "Deconstructing the Myth About al-Qa'ida and Khobar," *CTC Sentinel*, Vol. 1, No. 3, February 2008, pp. 20–22

Henderson, Simon, "The Elephant in the Gulf: The Arab States and Iran's Nuclear Program," Washington Institute for Near East Policy, Policy Watch 1065, 21 December 2005. As of 17 December 2008:
http://www.washingtoninstitute.org/templateC05.php?CID=2424

Herb, Michael, "Subordinate Communities and the Utility of Ethnic Ties to a Neighboring Regime: Iran and the Shi'a of the Arab States of the Gulf," in Leonard Binder, *Ethnic Conflict and International Politics of the Middle East,* Gainesville, Fl.: University Press of Florida Press, 1999.

"Hezbollah Takes Over West Beirut," *BBC News*, 9 May 2008.

"Hizballah's Nasrallah Discusses Recent War, Supports Army, UNIFIL Deployment," *New TV Channel* (Beirut), GMP20060828617001, 27 August 2006.

"Hizbollah 'Seizes West Beirut,'" *al-Jazeera*, 9 May 2008.

Hiltermann, Joost, "Iraq and the New Sectarianism in the Middle East," synopsis of a presentation at the Massachusetts Institute of Technology, 12 November 2006. As of 17 December 2008:
http://www.crisisgroup.org/home/index.cfm?id=4558

Hollis, Rosemary, "Whatever Happened to the Damascus Declaration," in M. Jane Davis, ed., *Politics and International Relations in the Middle East*, Aldershot, England: Edward Elgar, 1995.

House, Karen Elliot, "Saudi Balancing Act," *The Wall Street Journal*, 4 April 2007.

Hussein, Adnan al-Sayid, "Amn al-Khalij wa al-Malaf al-Nawawi wa al-Hiwar al-Arabi [Security of the Gulf, the Nuclear Portfolio, and the Arab-Iranian Dialogue]," *al-Hayat*, 10 February 2007.

Ibrahim, Foud, *The Shi'is of Saudi Arabia,* London, England: Dar al-Saqi, 2007.

International Crisis Group, "Bahrain's Sectarian Challenge," *ICG Middle East Report,* No. 40, Brussels: International Crisis Group, 6 May 2005a.

———, "The Shiite Question in Saudi Arabia," *Middle East Report,* No. 45, September 2005b.

International Energy Agency, "World Energy Outlook 2008." As of 10 February 2009:
http://www.worldenergyoutlook.org/2008.asp

Interview with King Abdullah, *al-Siyasa* (Kuwait), 27 January 2007.

"In the Most Recent Report by the Majlis Research Centre: Improving Relations with Saudi Arabia Can Increase Iranian Diplomacy's Negotiating Power Against West," *Aftab-e Yazd* (Tehran), translated by Open Source Center, IAP20070416011006, 16 April 2007.

"Iran," Press TV, 25 December 2008.

"Iran Admits Hurt by High Domestic Oil Consumption," Agence France Presse, 9 September 2007.

"Iran: Ahmadinejad Calls for Saudi Support to Fill Regional 'Power Vacuum,'" Open Source Center Feature: Iran, FEA20071004349826, 28 August–26 September 2007.

"Iran: Ahmadinezhad's Call for Elimination of Israel Continues to Stir Controversy," *Iran: Open Source Center Analysis,* IAF20070516573001, 16 May 2007.

"Iran: Cleric Says President's Trip to Mecca Sign of Iran's 'Popularity'" *Ahvaz Vision of the Islamic Republic of Iran Khuzestan Provincial TV,* translated by Open Source Center, IAP20071221950070, 21 December 2007.

"Iran Denies Discussing Israeli Ties with Saudis," *Gulf News*, 5 March 2007.

"Iran, Egypt Discuss Keeping Gaza Supply Route Open," Iran News Agency, 28 January 2008.

"Iran, Egypt Opt for Upgrading Ties," Iran News Agency, 26 January 2008.

"Iran, Malaysia, Syria, Venezuela Sign Refinery Deal," Fars News Agency, 1 November 2007.

"Iran Media Guide," BBC Monitoring (Caversham), translated by Open Source Center, IAP20070327950024, 27 March 2007.

"Iran, Russia, Qatar Mull Forming OPEC-Style Natural Gas Cartel," Associated Press, 21 October 2008.

"Iran, Saudi Arabia Open New Chapter in Regional Cooperation," Mehr News Agency (Tehran), translated by Open Source Center, IAP20060613950083, 13 June 2006.

"Iran: Shia, Sunni Clerics Call for Unity, Criticize Wahhabism," *Kermanshah Vision of the Islamic Republic of Iran Kermanshah Provincial TV,* translated by Open Source Center, IAP20080225434002, 23 February 2008.

"Iran Slams Arab, International Inaction over Gaza," Fars News Agency, 4 January 2009.

"Iran… The Password," editorial, *al-Watan* (Abha), translated by Open Source Center, GMP2006112827002, 21 November 2006.

"Iranian Daily: Theologians Concerned by Reported Sunni Preaching in Khuzestan," *Aftab-e Yazd* (Tehran), translated by Open Source Center, IAP20051221011046, 20 December 2005.

"Iranian Official Says Tehran Ready to Hold 'Multilateral' Talks with GCC Nations," Islamic Republic news agency (Tehran), translated by Open Source Center, IAP20051203011031, 3 December 2005.

"Iranian Pilgrims Reportedly Mistreated by Hardline Salafis," Tehran Raja News, translated by Open Source Center, IAP2008010101606001, 31 December 2007.

"Iranian Radio and TV Sets up Course for Afghan Journalists," Bakhtar Information Agency, supplied by BBC Monitoring: International Reports, 18 July 2003.

"Iranian-Saudi Row Reignites, Again Focusing on Pilgrimage Dispute," *Mideast Mirror*, Vol. 8, No. 52, March 16, 1994.

"Iran's Al-Alam TV Plays Role in Arab Media Scene," BBC Monitoring, translated by Open Source Center, FEA20070115074391, 15 January 2007.

"Iran's FM Mottaki on Nuke File, Larijani, US Threats, Shiite Crescent, Saudi Ties," *al-Dammam al-Yawm,* translated by Open Source Center, GMP20071126614006, 26 November 2007.

"Iran's Hard-Line President Ahmadinejad Tries to Pry Gulf Arabs Out of U.S. Alliance," Associated Press, 15 May 2007.

"Iran's President Ahmadinezhad Performs Hajj in Saudi Arabia," *Riyadh TV1,* Open Source Center Feature–Islamic Republic of Iran News Network, FEA20071223468867, 18–20 December 2007.

"Iran's Top Security Official Warns USA Against Attack," *Vision of the Islamic Republic of Iran Network,* 2 February 2005, 8 February 2004.

"Iraq, Saudi to Monitor Sectarian Fatwas," *The Peninsula*, 16 July 2007.

"Iraqi Sunni and Shiite Clerics Sign Peace Appeal in Mecca," *Agence France Press*, 20 October 2006.

"Iraq Television Viewership Poll," Department of State, Office of Intelligence and Research, 16 October 2003.

Jarous, Saud, "Syria Surprised by Saudi Reconciliation—Sources," *al-Sharq al-Awsat* (English), 22 January 2009.

Jehl, Douglas, "On Trip to Mend Ties, Iran's President Meets Saudi Prince," *The New York Times*, 17 May 1999.

"Jesarate padeshahe Bahrain be jazayere Irani! [Bahrain's King Impudence about the Iranian Islands!]," *Aftab News*, 18 December 2006. As of 21 December 2006: http://www.aftabnews.ir/vdcjyheuqxeii.html

Jones, Toby Craig, "The Iraq Effect in Saudi Arabia," *Middle East Report,* Vol. 237, Winter 2005. As of 21 April 2008:
http://www.merip.org/mer/mer237/jones.html

———, "Rebellion on the Saudi Periphery: Modernity, Marginalization and the Shia Uprising of 1979," *International Journal of Middle East Studies,* Vol. 38, 2006.

———, "Saudi Arabia's Not So New Anti-Shi'ism," *Middle East Report,* Vol. 242, Spring 2007.

Kahwaji, Riad, "Experts: Israel Should Back Up U.S. Arms for GCC," *Defense News,* 9 April 2007.

Kaye, Dalia Dassa, and Frederic M. Wehrey, "A Nuclear Iran: The Reactions of Neighbours," *Survival,* Vol. 49, No. 2, Summer 2007.

"Kayfa Yandhuru al-Arab ila Iran? [Panorama: How Do Arabs View Iran?]," *al-Arabia Television Network,* Panorama program, 26 February 2007. As of 19 December 2008:
http://www.alarabiya.net/programs/2007/02/26/32078.html

Kechichian, Joseph A., *Security Efforts in the Arab World: A Brief Examination of Four Regional Organizations,* Santa Monica, Calif.: RAND Corporation, N-3570-USDP, 1994. As of 19 December 2008:
http://www.rand.org/pubs/notes/N3570/

———, *Oman and the World: The Emergence of an Independent Foreign Policy,* Santa Monica, Calif.: RAND Corporation, MR-680-RC, 1995. As of February 10, 2009:
http://www.rand.org/pubs/monograph_reports/MR680/

———, "Reconciliation of Friendly Neighbors," *Gulf News,* 7 October 2007.

Keynoush, Banafsheh, *The Iranian-Saudi Arabian Relationship: From Ideological Confrontation to Pragmatic Accommodation,* doctoral dissertation at the Fletcher School of Law and Diplomacy, Tufts University, Medford, Mass., 2007.

Khalaji, Mehdi, "Apocalyptic Politics: On the Rationality of Iranian Policy," *Policy Focus,* No. 79, Washington, D.C.: Washington Institute for Near East Policy, 2008.

Khan, Ali, "Plan to Deal with Radiation Hazard Before Shoura Council," *Arab News,* 24 March 2008. As of 19 December 2008:
http://www.arabnews.com/?page=1&section=0&article=108173&d=24&m=3&y=2008

Khouri, Rami, "Four Days That Changed the Middle East," *The Daily Star,* 12 May 2008.

Knickmeyer, Ellen, "In Syria, Converting for Sake of Politics: Hezbollah's Gains During Lebanon War Inspire Sunnis to Become Shiis," *The Washington Post*, 6 October 2006.

Kraig, Michael "Assessing Alternative Security Frameworks for the Persian Gulf," *Middle East Policy*, Vol. 11, No. 3, fall 2004.

Kupchan, Charles, and Ray Takeyh, "Iran Just Won't Stay Isolated," *Los Angeles Times*, 4 March 2008. As of 2 April 2008: http://www.cfr.org/publication/15656/iran_just_wont_stay_isolated.html?breadcrumb=%2Fbios%2F9599%2F

"Kuwait News Agency—Concerns over Bushehr: Kuwait Raises Israeli Nukes," International Institute for Strategic Studies, 20 November 2006. As of 3 December 2008. http://www.iiss.org/whats-new/iiss-in-the-press/press-coverage-2006/november-2006/concerns-over-bushehr-kuwait-raises-israeli

"Kyrgyzstan Plans to Buy Iranian Wheat," Kyrgyz News Agency Web site *24.kg*, 2 October 2007.

"Kyrgyzstan, Iran Mull Joint Car Venture," Kyrgyz News Agency AKIpress, supplied by BBC Worldwide Monitoring, Middle East: Political Section, 1 July 2006.

"Kyrgyzstan, Iran Sign Cooperation Memorandum," Kyrgyz News Agency (Kabar), 21 August 2006.

"Kyrgyzstan, Iran Sign Protocol on Archives," Kyrgyz News Agency AKIpress, 25 February 2008.

"Kyrgyzstan: Saudi 'Businessman' Finances Construction of New Mosque," *Bishkek Kyrgyz Television*, translated by Open Source Center, CEP20050928027149, 28 September 2005.

"Last Syrian Troops Leave Lebanon," *CNN*, 27 April 2005.

"Latent Saudi-Iran Oil Price War Seen," APS Diplomatic News Service, 24 March 2008.

"Launching Six Saudi Satellites," Saudi Press Agency, 17 April 2007.

Lawson, Fred H., *Bahrain: The Modernization of Autocracy*, Boulder, Colorado: Westview Press, 1989, pp. 117–134.

"Leader's Representative: Iranians and Pakistanis Same Nation," Islamic Republic News Agency (Tehran), translated by Open Source Center, IAP20080310950116, 10 March 2008.

"Lebanon: Hezbollah's Outsourcing Strategy," *Strategic Forecasting Inc.*, 8 April 2008.

Leggett, Karby, and Marcus W. Brauchli, "Israelis Reach Out to Arab Nations That Share Fear of Ascendant Iran," *The Wall Street Journal*, 3 October 2006.

Legrenzi, Matteo, "The Peninsula Shield Force: End of a Symbol?" *Gulf Research Center Insights*, Issue 3, July 2006

———, "Mutual Threat Perceptions in the Gulf," *Middle East Policy*, Vol. 14, No. 2, Summer 2007.

Levitt, Matthew A., "Hezbollah: Financing Terror through Criminal Enterprise," testimony before the Committee on Homeland Security and Governmental Affairs, U.S. Senate, 25 May 2005.

———, "Iranian State Sponsorship of Terror: Threatening U.S. Security, Global Stability and Regional Peace," testimony before the U.S. House of Representatives Committee on International Relations, 16 February 2007.

Lippman, Thomas, "Saudi Arabia: The Calculations of Uncertainty," *The Nuclear Tipping Point*, Brookings Institution Press, 2004.

Logan, Kitty, "Iran Rebuilds Lebanon to Boost Hizbollah," *The Telegraph*, 31 July 2007.

Long, David E., "The Impact of the Iranian Revolution on the Arabian Peninsula and the Gulf States," in John L. Esposito, *The Iranian Revolution: Its Global Impact,* Miami: Florida International Press, 1990.

Louër, Laurence, *Transnational Shia Politics: Religious and Political Networks in the Gulf,* London, England: Hurst and Company, 2008.

Lowe, Robert, and Claire Spencer, eds., *Iran: Its Neighbors and the Regional Crises*, Royal Institute of International Affairs, Chatham House, 2006.

Lynch, Marc "Dueling Arab Summits," *Foreignpolicy.com*, 16 January 2009.

MacAskill, Ewen, and Chris McGreal, "Israel Should Be Wiped Off Map, Says Iran's President," *The Guardian*, 27 October 2005.

MacAskill, Ewen, and Ian Traynor, "Saudis Consider Nuclear Bomb," *The Guardian*, 18 September 2003. As of 19 December 2008: http://www.guardian.co.uk/saudi/story/0,11599,1044402,00.html

Mahfouz, Mohammad, ed., *al-Hiwar al-Madhhabi fi al-Mamlaka al-Arabiya al-Saudiya [Sectarian Dialogue in the Kingdom of Saudi Arabia],* Qatif, Saudi Arabia: Aafaq Center for Training and Studies, 2007.

Malbrunot, Georges, "Golf Alors que la tension monte entre Washington et Teheran: Les Chiites d'Arabie sous l'oeil de l'Iran [Gulf While Tension Rises Between Washington and Tehran: The Saudi Shiites Under the Watch of Iran]," *Le Figaro*, 17 November 2007.

"Mamuriat e jadid e America bray e Arabistan, Mesr, va Ordon [America's New Instructions for Saudi Arabia. Egypt, and Jordan]," Raja News, 24 April 2008.

Mansharof, Y., H. Varulkar, D. Lav, and Y. Carmon, "The Middle East on a Collision Course (4): Saudi/Sunni-Iranian/Shiite Conflict-Diplomacy and Proxy Wars," *Middle East Media Research Institute (MEMRI)*, Inquiry and Analysis Series, No. 324, 9 February 2007.

Mathee, Rudee, "The Egyptian Opposition on the Iranian Revolution," in Juan R. I. Cole and Nikki R. Keddie, *Shi'ism and Social Protest,* New Haven, Conn.: Yale University Press, 1986.

"Mavaze 14 Mars by mozoue Arabistan Saudi gereh khordeh [The Positions of March 14 Are Tied to the Saudi Position]," Fars News Agency, 29 April 2008. As of 19 December 2008:
http://www.farsnews.com/printable.php?nn=8702100945

Middle East Media Research Institute, "An Eternal Curse on the Muftis of the Saudi Court and on the Pharoah of Egypt," *Jomhouri-ye Eslami*, 28 July 2006.

———, "Recent Saudi-Iranian Contacts to Resolve the Lebanon Crisis," *Special Dispatch Series*, 26 January 2007.

Milani, Mohsen, "Iran's Gulf Policy: From Idealism and Confrontation to Pragmatism and Moderation," in Jamal S. al-Suwaidi, *Iran and the Gulf: A Search for Stability*, Abu Dhabi: Emirates Center for Strategic Studies and Research, 1996.

———, "Iran's Policy Toward Afghanistan," *Middle East Journal,* Vol. 60, No. 2, Spring 2006.

Moaveni, Azadeh, "Why Iran Isn't Cheering," *Time*, 23 July 2006.

"Moderation Within Salafi Stream," Abha *al-Watan,* Open Source Center Saudi Writer Notes Some Self-Criticism, GMP20071115614007, 15 November 2007. [Commentary by Hamzah Qabalan al-Mizyani: "More Self-Criticism"]

"Mokhalafat Arabistan ba eghdam nezami alayhe Iran [Saudi Arabia's Opposition to Military Attacks Against Iran]," Tabnak News, 18 April 2008. As of 19 December 2008: http://tabnak.ir/pages/print.php?cid=8151

Moran, Dominic, "The Golan, via Ankara," *International Relations and Security Networks*, 8 May 2008.

"Moshajreh Mottaki va Saud Al Faisal dar hashiye neshast Kuwait [Discussions Between Mottaki and Saud al-Faisal on the Margins of the Kuwait Meeting]," Tabnak News, 28 April 2008. As of 19 December 2008: http://tabnak.ir/pages/print.php?cid=9730

Nahas, Marida, "State-Systems and Revolutionary Challenge: Nasser, Khomeini and the Middle East," *International Journal of Middle East Studies*, Vol. 17, No. 4, November 1985.

Nahmias, Roee, "Mugniyah Murder Probe Points to Saudi Involvement," *YnetNews*, 9 April 2008a.

———, "Jumblatt: Iranian Flights to Beirut Transporting Arms for Hizbullah," *YnetNews*, 3 May 2008b.

———, "Report: Iran Building Communications System for Hizbullah," *YnetNews*, 4 May 2008c.

Naïm, Mouna, "Riyadh Solicits Damascus to Alleviate Lebanese Tensions," *Le Monde* (Paris; in French), 26 January 2007.

Nakash, Yizhak, *Reaching for Power: The Shi'a in the Modern Arab World*, Princeton, N.J.: Princeton University Press, 2006.

Nasr, Vali, *The Shi'a Revival: How Conflicts Within Islam Will Shape the Future*, New York: W.W. Norton, 2005.

"Nasrallah Interviewed on Lebanese Television," New TV Channel, Open Source Center Feature, FEA20060827026917, 27 August 2006.

"Nasrallah: Mughniyeh's Killers Must and Will Be Punished," *Jerusalem Post*, 24 March 2008.

"Negahi be sheklgiriye shoraye hamkariye khalije fars: Etehadi ke az jange Iran va aragh motevalled shod [A look at the establishment of the Persian Gulf Cooperation Council: A cooperation born as a result of Iran-Iraq war]," *Aftab News*, 7 July 2006. As of 19 December 2008: http://www.aftabnews.ir/vdca6en49anay.html

Nonneman, Gerd, "Determinants and Patterns of Saudi Foreign Policy: 'Omnibalancing' and 'Relative Autonomy' in Multiple Environments," in Paul Aarts and Gerd Nonneman, eds., *Saudi Arabia in the Balance: Political Economy, Society, Foreign Affairs*, New York: New York University Press, 2005, pp. 315–351.

Norton, Augustus Richard, "The Shiite 'Threat' Revisited," *Current History*, December 2007.

Noueihed, Lin, "Analysis-Gulf Arabs Chart Delicate Course Between Iran, U.S.," Reuters, 10 January 2008.

Obaid, Nawaf, "Regional Ramifications of the Lebanon Ceasefire: A Saudi View," Saudi-US Relations Information Service, 27 September 2006a.

———, "Stepping into Iraq: Saudi Arabia Will Protect Sunnis If the U.S. Leaves," *The Washington Post*, 26 November 2006b.

Office of the Director National Intelligence and the National Intelligence Council, *Iran: Nuclear Intentions and Capabilities*, November 2007.

Okruhlik, Gwen, "Saudi Arabian-Iranian Relations: External Rapprochement and Internal Consolidation," *Middle East Policy*, Vol. 10, No. 2, Summer 2003.

"OPEC Blunder Reveals Saudi-Iran Disagreement on Dollar," *Agence France-Presse*, 17 November 2007.

Open Source Center, Persian Press: Commentary Argues Saudis Seek Improved Ties with Rafsanjani Visit; IAP20080616011005 Tehran *Hamshahri* in Persian 11 Jun 08 p 17 [Unattributed commentary from the "Politics" column: "Outcome of Rafsanjani's Saudi Visit"].

Ottaway, Marina, "The New Arab Diplomacy: Not with the U.S. and Not Against the U.S.," *Carnegie Papers*, Number 94, Washington, D.C.: Carnegie Endowment for International Peace, July 2008.

"Parliament Speaker Condemns Desecration of Shiites' Shrines," Fars News Agency, 13 June 2007.

Parsi, Trita, "Israel and the Origins of Iran's Arab Option: Dissection of a Strategy Misunderstood," *Middle East Journal*, Vol. 60, No. 3, Summer 2006.

Partrick, Neil, "Dire Straits for US Mideast Policy: The Gulf Arab States and US-Iran Relations," *Royal United Services Institute Commentary*, 9 January 2008. As of 19 December 2008:
http://www.rusi.org/research/studies/menap/commentary/ref:C4784DF6A9E6B2/

Peterson, Scott, "Saudi Arabia, Iran Target Mideast's Sectarian Discord," *Christian Science Monitor*, 5 March 2007.

Pollack, Kenneth, "Securing the Gulf," *Foreign Affairs*, Vol. 83, No. 4, 2003.

Prados, Alfred B., and Christopher M. Blanchard, *Saudi Arabia: Current Issues and U.S. Relations*, CRS Report for Congress, Washington, D.C.: Congressional Research Service, 9 January 2007.

President Ahmadinejad's statements in the Islamic Republic News Agency, 1 April 2007.

Paris, Gilles, "Quand la diplomatie saoudienne s'active [Saudi Diplomacy Is Becoming Proactive]," Le Monde (Paris; in French), 10 February 2007.

Qusti, Raid, "GCC to Confront Iraq Security Fallout," *Arab News*, 4 July 2007. As of 17 December 2008:
http://arabnews.com/?page=4&section=0&article=98169&d=4&m=7&y=2007

Rashid, Ahmed, *Taliban: Militant Islam, Oil and Fundamentalism in Central Asia*, New Haven, Conn.: Yale University Press, 2000.

Rasul, Muhammad, *Al-Wahhabiyyun wa al-'Iraq [The Wahhabis and Iraq]*, Beirut: Riad el-Rayyes Books, 2005.

Rathmell, Andrew, Theodore W. Karasik, and David C. Gompert, *A New Persian Gulf Security System*, Santa Monica, Calif.: RAND Corporation, IP-248-CMEPP, 2003. As of 19 December 2008:
http://www.rand.org/pubs/issue_papers/IP248/

"Report of the Fact-Finding Mission to Lebanon," 24 March 2005.

"Report of the International Independent Investigation Commission Established Pursuant to Security Council Resolution 1595," 20 October 2005

Research Institute of Strategic Studies, "Bohran-e Aragh va payamadhaye manfiye an bar amniyat va manafe melli jomhouriye eslamiye Iran [Iraq's Crisis and Its Negative Consequences on Iran's Security and National Interests]," 2003.

"Riyadh Accused of Role in Mughniyeh Assassination," *Daily Star*, 10 April 2008.

"Riyadh Backs Iran N. Program," Fars News Agency, 20 June 2007.

Ross, Dennis, "Statecraft in the Middle East," *Washington Quarterly*, Summer 2008.

Roth, John, Douglas Greenburg, and Serena Wilde, "Terrorist Financing Staff Monograph," National Commission on Terrorist Attacks Upon the United States, 2004. As of 17 December 2008:
http://govinfo.library.unt.edu/911/staff_statements/index.htm

Rougier, Bernard, *Everyday Jihad: The Rise of Militant Islam Among Palestinians in Lebanon*, Cambridge, Mass.: Harvard University Press, 2007.

Rousselin, Pierre, "Hezbollah's Coup d'Etat [Hezbollah's Strike to the State], *Le Figaro* (Paris), 9 May 2008.

Roy, Olivier, *The Failure of Political Islam*, Cambridge, Mass.: Harvard Belknap Press, 2001.

Russell, James A., "Whither Regional Security in a World Turned Upside Down?" *Middle East Policy*, Vol. 14, No. 2, Summer 2007.

Russell, Richard L., "Peering Over the Horizon: Arab Threat Perception and Security Responses to a Nuclear-Ready Iran," Non-Proliferation Policy Education Center, 5 February 2005a.

Russell, Richard, "The Collective Security Mirage," *Middle East Policy*, Vol. 12, No. 4, 2005b.

"Ruyarui-e Iran va Arabestan dar khavar-e miane [Iran and Saudi Arabia Confrontation in the Middle East]," *Aftab News*, 5 December 2006. As of 19 December 2008:
http://www.aftabnews.ir/vdchkqn23znkm.html

Ryan, Curtis, *Jordan in Transition: From Hussein to Abdullah*, Boulder, Colo.: Lynne Rienner Press, 2002.

———, "The Odd Couple: Ending the Jordanian-Syrian 'Cold War,'" *Middle East Journal*, Vol. 60, No. 1, Winter 2006.

Saad-Ghorayeb, Amal, *Hizbu'llah: Politics and Religion*, Sterling, Va.: Pluto Press, 2002.

Sadjadpour, Karim, "The Nuclear Players," *Journal of International Affairs*, Vol. 60, No. 2, Spring/Summer 2007.

————, *Reading Khamenei: Reading Khamenei: The World View of Iran's Most Powerful Leader*, Washington, D.C.: Carnegie Endowment, March 2008. As of 18 December 2008:
http://www.carnegieendowment.org/files/sadjadpour_iran_final2.pdf

Sapsted, David, "Doha Commended on Lebanon Agreement," *The National*, 22 May 2008.

"Saudi Arabia Backs Extraordinary Arab League Meeting on Lebanon," *Arab News*, 9 May 2008.

"Saudi Arabia Dislikes High-Level Gaza Summit," Press TV, 14 January 2009.

"Saudi Arabia: Report on Arrests in Eastern Region for Sympathezing with Hizballah" (Unattributed report from Qatif: "In al-Qatif, a number of sons of the region arrested), translated by Open Source Center, GMP2006101866001, 15 October 2006.

"Saudi Authorities Close Down Shi'ite Mosque in al-Ihsa Governorate" (al-Rasid report by Muhammad Ali in al-Munayzilah headed: "Security authorities close mosque in village of al-Munayzilah"), translated by Open Source Center, GMP20061003866002, 2 October 2006.

"Saudi Daily Views Heated Debate Between Clerics on Shiite Threat, Hizballah," *al-Watan* (Abha), translated by Open Source Center, GMP2006092814005, 28 September 2006.

"Saudi Development Fund Agrees to Finance Express Road in Northern Lebanon," Saudi Press Agency (Riyadh), GMP20061016831004, 16 October 2006.

"Saudi Editorial: Nasrallah's Statement Proves Saudi Stand on Lebanon War Sound," *al-Watan* (Abha), translated by Open Source Center, GMP20060829614007, 29 August 2006.

"Saudi Foreign Minister on Lebanon, Iraq, Sectarian Issues," *al-Arabiya Television*, Open Source Center Feature, FEA20070129084306, 25 January 2007.

"Saudi Mufti Lists Reasons for Warning Youths against Seeking Jihad Abroad," Saudi Press Agency (Riyadh), translated by Open Source Center, GMP20071002825008, 1 October 2007.

"Saudi Reportedly Funding Iraqi Sunnis," Associated Press, 8 December 2006.

"Saudi Shiite Cleric Supports Call for Harmony Between Shiites, Sunnis in Iraq" [Article by Hasan al-Saffar: "The Sectarian Sedition in Iraq Under Gulf's Necessity of Unity and Importance of Dialogue and Harmony"], *al-Risalah* (Jedda), translated by Open Source Center, GMP20070127614003, 19 January 2007.

"Saudi Wahhabis Reportedly Funding Wahhabi Communities in Iran," Persian Press, [Report citing Jahan News Agency: "Wahhabis investing heavily in southern Iran"], Hezbollah (Tehran), translated by Open Source Center, IAP20071007011005, 2 October 2007.

"Saudi Warns Lebanon Opposition Against Escalation," *Agence France Presse*, 8 May 2008.

"Saudis Say Iran No Threat," Press TV, 7 July 2007. As of 19 December 2008: http://www.presstv.com/detail.aspx?id=15638&sectionid=351020205

Schenker, David, *Saudi-Iranian Mediation on Hizballah: Will a Lebanon Deal Come at Syria's Expense*, Policy Watch 1204, Washington, D.C.: The Washington Institute for Near East Policy, February 2007.

————, *Beyond Rhetoric: Hizballah Threats After the Mughniyeh Assassination*, Washington, D.C.: The Washington Institute for Near East Policy, 28 February 2008.

Schneider, Howard, "Saudi Pact with Iran is Sign of Growing Trust," *The Washington Post*, 17 April 2001.

Semple, Kirk, "Sunni Leaders Say U.S.-Iran Talks Amount to Meddling," *The New York Times*, 18 March 2006.

Shai, Shaul, *The Axis of Evil: Iran, Hizballah, and the Palestinian Terror*, Piscataway, N.J.: Transaction Books, 2005.

"Shart ajib e Saudiha baraye bazgashti sefarat dar Baghdad [The Saudis' Strange Condition for the Return of Their Embassy to Baghdad]," Tabnak News, 9 April 2008. As of 19 December 2008: http://tabnak.ir/pages/print.php?cid=9422

"Shaykh Salman al-Awda Warns of Sectarian War in Iraq, Holds the US Responsible," *Islam Today*, translated by Open Source Center, GMP20061107866002, 5 November 2006.

Shihri, Abdullah, "Clerics Urge Muslims to Back Iraq Sunnis," Associated Press, 12 December 2006.

Shobokshi, Hussein, "Lebanon: Before It Disappears," *Al-Sharq Al-Awsat*, 7 May 2008.

"Shoray e hamkari khalij fars Israel ra masool fajayat e navar Ghaz e danest [The Persian Gulf Cooperation Council Accused Israel of the Gaza Tragedy]," Fars News Agency, 28 April 2008. As of 19 December 2008: http://www.farsnews.com/printable.php?nn=8702090586

Slackman, Michael, "Iran and Saudi Arabia Mediating in Lebanon Crisis," *International Herald Tribune*, 30 January 2007a.

————, "Iran and Saudi Arabia Mediate in Lebanon Crisis as U.S. Looks on," *The New York Times*, 31 January 2007b.

Slackman, Michael M., and Hassan M. Fattah, "In Public View, Saudis Counter Iran in Region," *The New York Times*, 6 February 2007.

Smith, Michael, "Iran Threatens Gulf Blitz If U.S. Hits Nuclear Plant" *The Times* (London), 10 June 2007.

Solomon, Jay, "Religious Divide: To Contain Iran, U.S. Seeks Help from Arab Allies," *The Wall Street Journal*, 24 November 2006.

"Special Report: Saudi Arabia," *Middle East Economic Digest*, Vol. 52, No. 8, 22–28 February 2008.

Stack, Megan, "Hands Off or Not? Saudis Wring Theirs Over Iraq," *The New York Times*, 24 May 2006.

Stracke, Nicole, "Nuclear Development in the Gulf: A Strategic or Economic Necessity," *Security and Terrorism Research Bulletin*, Gulf Research Center, No. 7, December 2007.

Stuart, Douglas T., and William T. Tow, *China, the Soviet Union, and the West: Strategic and Political Dimensions in the 1980s,* Boulder, Colo.: Westview Press, 1982.

"Sunni Rising: The Growth of Sunni Militancy in Lebanon," *Jane's Intelligence Review*, 5 December 2007.

"Surprise Reconciliation at Kuwait Summit," *The National* (UAE), 21 January 2009.

"Syria's Al-Shu'aybi: Olmert Agreement to Return Golan Meets Al-Asad Conditions," London Quds Press, translated by Open Source Center, GMP20080424632004, 24 April 2008.

"Taghier negrash nesbat beh barbame atomi Iran [A Change in the Level of Anxiety Among Arabs Regarding Iran's Nuclear Program]," *Tabnak.ir*, 15 April 2008. As of 19 December 2008: http://tabnak.ir/pages/print.php?cid=9111

Takeyh, Ray, *Hidden Iran: Paradox and Power in the Islamic Republic,* New York: Times Books, 2007.

Teitelbaum, Joshua, "Has the Shiite Crescent Disappeared? Saudi Arabia and the U.S. Alliance," *Tel Aviv Notes*, The Moshe Dayan Center, Tel Aviv University, 27 January 2007.

Telhami, Shibley, "2008 Annual Arab Public Opinion Poll," Survey of the Anwar Sadat Chair for Peace and Development at the University of Maryland (with Zogby International), March 2008.

Telhami, Shibley, and Michael N. Barnett, eds., *Identity and Foreign Policy Formulation in the Middle East,* New York: Cornell University Press, January 2002.

"Tensions Increase Between Iran and Saudi Arabia," *Power and Interest News Report,* 19 January 2007.

Thom, William G., "Trends in Soviet Support for African Liberation," *Air University Review,* July–August 1974.

Timmerman, Kenneth R., "The Saudi-Iranian Thaw," *The Wall Street Journal,* 26 May 1999.

Trevelyan, Mark, "Gulf Arabs See Israel Stopping Iran Bomb," Reuters, 8 February 2008.

"Trilateral Talks Rattle Gulf States While Concealing Complex Iranian Dynamics," *Gulf States Newsletter,* Vol. 31, No. 807, 8 June 2007.

"UK Daily Views Gulf Arabs' Dilemma Over Response to Iran's Suspected Ambitions, London," *The Financial Times,* EUP20070102167006, 1 January 2007.

United Nations, *Report of the Fact-Finding Mission to Lebanon Inquiring into the Causes, Circumstances and Consequences of the Assassination of Former Prime Minister Rafik Hariri, 25 February–24 March 2005* (also known as the Fitzgerald Report), 24 March 2005a.

———, *Report of the International Independent Investigation Commission Established Pursuant to Security Council Resolution 1595 (2005)* (also known as the Mehlis Report), October 2005b.

United Nations Security Council, "Security Council Demands Iran Suspend Uranium Enrichment by 31 August, or Face Possible Economic, Diplomatic Sanctions," 21 July 2006

U.S. Department of Energy, Energy Information Administration, Country Analysis Briefs, August 2008. As of 10 February 2009: http://www.eia.doe.gov/cabs/Region_me.html

"Vagraye Arab dar conference Dameshgh [Arab Opinions at Damascus Conference]," *Al Alam News,* 2 April 2008.

Valbjørn, Morten, and André Bank, "Signs of a New Arab Cold War: The 2006 Lebanon War and the Sunni-Shi'i Divide," *Middle East Report,* Spring 2007.

Vatanka, Alex, "The Making of an Insurgency in Iran's Balochistan Province," *Jane's Intelligence Review,* 1 June 2006.

———, "Iran's Shi'a Reach Out to Mainstream Salafists," *CTC Sentinel,* Vol. 1, No. 7, June 2008.

Verma, Sonia, "Iraq Could Have Largest Oil Reserves in the World," *The Times* (UK), 20 May 2008.

Wehrey, Frederic M., "Saudi Arabia: Shi'a Pessimistic on Reform, but Seek Reconciliation," Carnegie Endowment for International Peace, *Arab Reform Bulletin*, June 2007.

Windrem, Robert, "Are Saudis Waging an Oil-Price War on Iran?" *MSNBC*, January 26, 2007.

Worth, Robert F., "Al-Jazeera No Longer Nips at the Saudis," *The New York Times*, 4 January 2008.

"Writer Criticizes Al-Zawahiri's 'Sudden' Interest in Lebanon in Latest Message," al-Jazeera Talk (Doha), translated by Open Source Center, GMP20080425641002, 24 April 2008.

Yaphe, Judith S., and Charles D. Lutes, *Reassessing the Implications of a Nuclear-Armed Iran*, McNair Paper 69, Washington, D.C.: National Defense University, 2005.

Yasin, Kamal Nazer, "Iran: Political and Religious Leaders Play the Nationalist Card," *Eurasia Insight*, 19 April 2007. As of 17 December 2008:
http://www.eurasianet.org/departments/insight/articles/eav041907.shtml

Zahlan, Rosemarie Said, *The Making of the Modern Gulf States: Kuwait, Bahrain, Qatar, the United Arab Emirates and Oman*, London, England: Ithaca Press, 1998, pp. 135–155.

"Zionists, Occupiers Behind Samarra Crime, Says Leader," Islamic Republic News Agency, 14 June 2007.

Zogby International, "Middle East Opinion: Iran Fears Aren't Hitting the Arab Street," 2006. As of 19 December 2008:
http://www.zogby.com/Soundbites/Readclips.dbm?ID=14570